The
Keepsake Quilting™
COOKBOOK

THE FABRIC OF OUR LIVES®

The

Keepsake Quilting™
COOKBOOK

This cookbook is a collection of favorite recipes,
which are not necessarily original.

Published and Copyright © 2001
by Keepsake Quilting, Inc.
Route 25B
P.O. Box 1618
Center Harbor, New Hampshire 03226-1618
1-800-865-9458

Library of Congress Catalog Number: 00-093180
ISBN: 0-9704130-0-9

Edited, Designed, and Manufactured by
Favorite Recipes® Press
an imprint of

FRP

P. O. Box 305142, Nashville, Tennessee 37230
800-358-0560

Managing Editor: Mary Cummings
Art Director: Steve Newman
Cover and Book Design: Jim Scott
Book Project Managers: Georgia Brazil, Mary Wilson

First Printing: 2001   10,000 copies

DEDICATION

The *Keepsake Quilting Cookbook* is dedicated to all the women who have come before, whose recipes and quilts have enriched the lives of all of us who have followed.

These women answered their families' needs for food and warmth. They took vegetables, grains, meats, and spices and created a lifetime of healthful meals. They took fabric and thread and fashioned them into quilts and clothing for warmth and protection. Through it all, they added the priceless ingredients of their lives—their heritage and traditions, their talents and unique personalities—to create both meals and quilts that nourished the bodies and the souls of those they held dear.

We dedicate this book to them in grateful recognition of their silent achievements and unsung contributions.

TABLE OF CONTENTS

PREFACE

Keepsake Quilting, located in the scenic town of Center Harbor, New Hampshire, is the largest quilt shop in America. Its mail-order catalog reaches quilters all around the world, providing them with fabrics, patterns, books, notions, and inspiration.

In the quiltmakers' tradition of caring and sharing, quilters from around the country and across the globe eagerly contributed favorite recipes to make this cookbook possible. All profits will be used to support charitable programs benefiting women and children in this country and worldwide.

We are especially grateful that, through the generosity of our contributors and your purchase of this book, together we truly can make a difference in the lives of women and children in need.

INTRODUCTION

For countless generations, recipes and quilt patterns have been shared with others, creating vital links that connect us to family, community, and heritage. Marvelous transformations occur as recipes and patterns are interpreted and adapted to reflect the lifestyle and individuality of each cook and quilter.

With this book, we celebrate the creativity, artistry, and self-expression of women who take the same basic ingredients, be they food or fabric, and transform them into creations that are uniquely their own. Whether they prepare a simple everyday meal or a gourmet holiday dinner, stitch a utility quilt or an award-winning showstopper, by adding their personal touch they expand and enhance their art. At the same time they realize the glowing sense of pride and satisfaction that comes from creating something that never was—something uniquely their own.

The recipes collected in this book reflect the diversity of both the women and the regions from which they come—New England, the Deep South, the Midwest, the Southwest, the West Coast, and far beyond the borders of the United States. Many have been handed down from grandmothers and great-grandmothers who immigrated to America with few belongings but with countless family recipes etched in their memories.

In quilting, as in cooking, basic ingredients lead to endless possibilities. The quilts that illustrate this book are all based on a single quilt block, *Stargazey Heartz,* designed by Australian quiltmaker Jan Mullen. It is a simple heart pattern, but it becomes many different quilts, each strikingly unique, when sewn in different sizes, settings, colors, and fabrics. From the look of scrap quilts of the mid-1800s to the simplicity of early twentieth-century Amish quilts and the innovative style of quilts of the twenty-first century, each has a unique voice, yet they retain the common thread of their design.

Through this cookbook and the recipes, quilts, and inspirational sayings gathered within it, we honor the traditions and ties that bind us and celebrate the individuality that sets us apart.

ACKNOWLEDGEMENTS

Cookbook Committee

Bonnie B. Knott
Beth H. Miller
Judy Sprague Sabanek
Russell A. Sabanek
Stephanie L. Smith

We gratefully thank the members of the Keepsake Quilting staff
who donated their time to kitchen test the recipes included in this book.

Quiltmakers

Jan Mullen
Bonnie B. Knott
Ellen Peters

A special thank-you to Jan Mullen for the use
of her *Stargazey Heartz* quilt pattern

and

to Cotton Incorporated for the use of
THE FABRIC OF OUR LIVES®.

BEGINNINGS

Heritage Hearts Quilt
42" × 51"

Nineteenth-century America was a period of enormous transition. The Civil War and the westward pioneer movement both changed the face of America forever. Women turned to quilting during this time of great upheaval in their lives. Stitched into the quilts of the 1800s are the pain and sorrow, the hopes and dreams of our quilting ancestors.

During the Civil War, women took part in the war effort by sending quilts to the soldiers. With each quilt went thoughts and prayers for their husbands, fathers, and sons far away from home. The pioneer movement brought the pain of separation from home, family, and lifelong friendships in the search for a new life. A quote from a pioneer woman's diary speaks volumes about the times—"I made quilts as fast as I could to keep my family warm, and as pretty as I could to keep my heart from breaking."

ARTICHOKE DIP

*Keep the golden brown top pretty for a nice presentation by
blotting lightly with a paper towel before serving.*

1 (14-ounce) can artichoke hearts
1 (5-ounce) wedge Parmesan cheese

1 cup mayonnaise
3 to 5 garlic cloves, minced

Drain the artichoke hearts and squeeze to remove excess moisture. Grate the Parmesan cheese.
Combine the artichoke hearts, cheese, mayonnaise and minced garlic in a bowl and mix well.
Spread the mixture in a l9-inch round baking dish. Bake at 375 degrees for 20 to 25 minutes
or until golden brown. Serve the dip hot with whole wheat crackers. Do not substitute
mayonnaise-type salad dressing for the mayonnaise in this recipe.

YIELD: 12 SERVINGS

BLACK BEAN SALSA

*Reserve a few sprigs of cilantro to use for a spritely garnish.
Warming the tortilla chips is a nice touch.*

2 (15-ounce) cans black beans
1 (15-ounce) can whole kernel corn
2 large tomatoes
1 large avocado
1/4 cup lime juice
1/2 red onion, chopped

1/4 cup chopped fresh cilantro
2 tablespoons light olive oil
2 tablespoons red wine vinegar
1 teaspoon salt (optional)
1/2 teaspoon pepper
Hot pepper sauce to taste

Drain the black beans, rinse and drain well. Place in a large bowl. Drain the corn and add to
the beans. Seed the tomatoes and chop into small pieces. Add to the bowl. Peel and seed the
avocado and chop into small pieces. Place the avocado in a small bowl, add the lime juice and
mix gently to coat with the lime juice and prevent browning. Add the avocado with the lime
juice to the bean mixture. Add the onion, cilantro, olive oil, vinegar, salt, pepper and hot
pepper sauce to the bean mixture and mix gently. Refrigerate, covered, until serving time. Place
the mixture in a serving bowl. Garnish with avocado slices dipped in lime or lemon juice.
Serve with tortilla chips.

YIELD: 18 TO 20 SERVINGS

SALSA CHEESE DIP

This recipe is still great even if you use low-fat products.

8 ounces cream cheese, softened
1 cup mild chunky salsa

1 cup shredded Cheddar cheese

Combine the cream cheese and salsa in a bowl and mix until no white chunks of cream cheese remain. Add the Cheddar cheese and mix well. Serve with tortilla chips.

YIELD: 8 SERVINGS

CREAMY SPINACH DIP

Use a food processor for quick preparation, but leave the mixture slightly chunky.
The dip will keep for up to a week in the refrigerator.

1 (10-ounce) package frozen chopped
   spinach, thawed
1/2 cup chopped green onions or
   scallions
1/2 cup chopped fresh parsley

1 teaspoon salt
1/4 teaspoon pepper
1/2 teaspoon dillweed
1 cup reduced-fat mayonnaise
1 cup reduced-fat sour cream

Drain the spinach and squeeze to remove the excess moisture. Combine the spinach, green onions, parsley, salt, pepper and dillweed in a mixing bowl. Add the mayonnaise and sour cream and mix well. Chill, covered, until serving time. Serve with an assortment of bite-size fresh vegetables such as broccoli, cauliflower, whole green beans, endive, cucumber slices, snow peas, zucchini and carrot sticks and green, red and yellow bell pepper strips.

YIELD: 10 TO 12 SERVINGS

He who sows courtesy, reaps friendship.
And he who plants kindness, gathers love.

COCKTAIL CRAB DIP

16 ounces cream cheese, softened
2 (6-ounce) cans crab meat

Cocktail sauce

Mix the cream cheese in a bowl until smooth and creamy. Drain the crab meat well and chop or flake if necessary. Add to the cream cheese and mix well. Shape the mixture into a loaf on a serving platter. Pour the desired amount of a favorite cocktail sauce over the top. Serve with an assortment of crackers.

YIELD: 20 TO 24 SERVINGS

SWEET AND PUNGENT DIP

1 (9-ounce) can crushed pineapple
1/2 cup finely chopped green
   bell pepper
1/3 cup finely chopped pimentos
1 garlic clove, minced
1/2 cup sugar

3 tablespoons soy sauce
3 generous dashes of Tabasco sauce
1/2 cup vinegar
1/2 cup water
2 tablespoons cornstarch

Combine the undrained pineapple, green pepper, pimentos, garlic, sugar, soy sauce, Tabasco sauce, vinegar and water in a medium saucepan. Bring the mixture to a boil. Blend the cornstarch with a few drops of water and stir into the hot mixture. Boil for 1 minute, stirring constantly. Serve the dip warm with an assortment of bite-size fresh vegetables or peeled cooked shrimp.

YIELD: 10 TO 12 SERVINGS

Those who bring sunshine to the lives of others cannot
keep it from themselves.

—*James Barrie*

Goat Cheese with Bell Pepper Dressing

1/4 cup chopped green bell pepper
1/4 cup chopped red bell pepper
1/4 cup chopped yellow bell pepper
1 tablespoon olive oil
4 large garlic cloves, thinly sliced
2 teaspoons minced fresh rosemary, or
  3/4 teaspoon dried
1/2 teaspoon coriander seeds, crushed
1/4 teaspoon fennel seeds, crushed

1/4 teaspoon ground pepper
1/4 teaspoon dried thyme
1 bay leaf
3 tablespoons olive oil
Salt to taste
8 ounces goat cheese such as
  Montrachet cheese, chilled
2 tablespoons toasted pine nuts

Sauté the bell peppers in 1 tablespoon olive oil in a heavy skillet over medium heat for 5 minutes or until tender. Reduce the heat to medium-low and add the garlic, rosemary, coriander seeds, fennel seeds, pepper, thyme, bay leaf and 3 tablespoons olive oil and mix well. Simmer for 5 minutes. Remove from the heat and add salt. Let stand until cooled to room temperature. Discard the bay leaf.

Cut the goat cheese into 8 slices and arrange the slices on a serving plate. Spoon the bell pepper dressing over the cheese slices. Let stand at room temperature for 1 hour. Sprinkle with the pine nuts. Serve with baguette slices or crackers.

YIELD: 4 SERVINGS

Jalapeño Cheese Ball

Leftovers are wonderful melted on toast.

1 pound sharp Cheddar or Monterey
  Jack cheese
5 jalapeño peppers
1 large onion

3 garlic cloves
1/2 cup mayonnaise
1 cup chopped almonds, walnuts or
  pecans

Shred the cheese into a large bowl. Remove the tops and seeds from the jalapeños and cut the onion into quarters. Combine the jalapeños, onion and garlic in a food processor and process until finely chopped. Add to the shredded cheese. Add the mayonnaise and mix well. Chill the mixture until firm enough to shape into a ball and roll in the chopped almonds to coat. Place on a serving plate and serve with tortilla chips or crackers.

YIELD: 10 TO 12 SERVINGS

TRIPLE-CHEESE SPREAD

Purchase the cheeses already shredded and preparation time can be less than 15 minutes.

8 ounces Monterey Jack cheese
8 ounces Cheddar cheese
8 ounces Velveeta cheese
1 onion, chopped
1 green bell pepper, chopped
1 tablespoon minced pimentos

2 cups mayonnaise
2 tablespoons sugar
2 tablespoons prepared mustard
2 dashes of Tabasco sauce
Salt and garlic salt to taste

Shred the cheeses and combine in a large bowl. Add the onion, green pepper and pimentos and toss until well mixed. Combine the mayonnaise, sugar, mustard, Tabasco sauce, salt and garlic salt in a small bowl and blend well. Add to the cheese mixture and mix well. Chill, covered, until serving time. Serve with assorted cocktail breads or crisp crackers, or spread on thinly sliced bread to cut into interesting shapes to serve as cocktail sandwiches.

YIELD: 12 TO 14 SERVINGS

CRAB MOUSSE

1 envelope unflavored gelatin
3 tablespoons cold water
1 (10-ounce) can cream of mushroom
  soup
8 ounces cream cheese, softened

$^3/_4$ cup mayonnaise
1 (6-ounce) can crab meat
1 cup chopped celery
1 small onion, finely chopped

Sprinkle the dry gelatin over the cold water. Let stand for several minutes until the gelatin is softened. Heat the soup in a saucepan but do not boil. Remove from the heat and add the softened gelatin and stir until the gelatin dissolves. Add the cream cheese and mix until well blended. Blend in the mayonnaise. Drain the crab meat well. Add the crab meat, celery and onion to the soup mixture and mix well.

Spoon the mixture into a lightly oiled gelatin mold. Chill, covered with plastic wrap, for 12 hours. Invert the mousse onto a serving plate. Surround the mousse with fresh parsley sprigs and top with a small sprig. Serve with assorted crackers.

YIELD: 10 TO 12 SERVINGS

SMOKED SALMON SPREAD

8 ounces cream cheese, softened
1/2 cup sour cream
3 tablespoons fresh lemon juice
1/2 cup finely chopped onion

1/4 cup finely chopped parsley
1 garlic clove, pressed or minced
Pepper to taste
8 ounces smoked salmon

Blend the cream cheese and sour cream in a mixing bowl. Add the lemon juice, onion, parsley, garlic and pepper and mix well. Shred the salmon. Add to the cream cheese mixture and mix lightly. Serve with assorted crackers or thinly sliced bread cut into triangles.

YIELD: 10 TO 12 SERVINGS

TAPENADE À LA PROVENÇE

This traditional olive paste or spread can also be prepared using green olives.

5 large garlic cloves
1 (6- or 7-ounce) can pitted
    black olives
1 tablespoon capers

2 flat anchovy fillets
1 1/2 tablespoons lemon juice
2 tablespoons olive oil
Freshly ground pepper to taste

Place the garlic in a food processor container and process until finely chopped. Add 3/4 of the olives and process until the consistency of a rough paste. Add the capers and anchovies and pulse until well mixed. Add the remaining olives and process to the desired consistency, which can be a fine paste or chunky spread. Remove the mixture to a bowl. Add the lemon juice, olive oil and pepper and mix well. Serve on crunchy bread.

YIELD: 8 TO 12 SERVINGS

The ornament of a house is the friends that frequent it.

—*Ralph Waldo Emerson*

NUTTY VEGETABLE PÂTÉ

Lovely as a filling in sandwiches or buns and yummy on crackers or biscuits,
but especially delicious served with a selection of crudités.

7 tablespoons butter
1 medium onion, finely chopped
2 garlic cloves, crushed
2 ribs celery, finely chopped
3 tablespoons flour
8 ounces button mushrooms

Juice of 1 lemon
1¹/₂ teaspoons instant chicken bouillon
¹/₄ cup tomato paste
Pepper to taste
¹/₂ red bell pepper, finely chopped
1 cup roasted cashews

Combine the butter, onion, garlic and celery in a microwave-safe bowl. Microwave on High for 4 minutes, stirring once. Add the flour and mix well. Microwave on High for 1 minute.

Reserve 1 mushroom for garnish. Chop the remaining mushrooms finely. Add the mushrooms, lemon juice, instant bouillon, tomato paste and pepper to the onion mixture and mix well. Microwave on High for 3 minutes.

Add the red bell pepper. Chop half the cashews finely and add to the mixture, mixing well. Microwave on High for 3 minutes.

Pour the mixture into 2 serving bowls. Slice the reserved mushroom thinly and arrange the slices over the top. Sprinkle with the remaining cashews. Chill, covered, until set.

YIELD: 2 CUPS

Cheerfulness and contentment are great beautifiers and
are famous preservers of youthful looks.

—*Charles Dickens*

MARINATED ASPARAGUS

*In a pinch, use two cans of asparagus spears. Just drain
well and proceed—no cooking needed.*

1¹/2 pounds fresh asparagus spears
1 green bell pepper, chopped
1 small bunch green onions with tops,
  chopped

1 rib celery, chopped
Paprika Dressing

Snap the tough ends from the asparagus. Place the asparagus in a steamer basket over boiling water. Steam, covered, for 6 to 8 minutes or just until tender-crisp. Drain well and place the warm asparagus, green pepper, green onions and celery in a large container with a lid.

Pour the Paprika Dressing over the vegetables. Chill, covered, for 4 hours or longer. Drain and place on a serving platter. Garnish with pimento strips.

YIELD: 6 SERVINGS

PAPRIKA DRESSING

¹/2 cup sugar
¹/4 teaspoon paprika
1 teaspoon salt

1 small garlic clove, minced
¹/2 cup red wine vinegar
³/4 cup vegetable oil

Combine the sugar, paprika, salt, garlic and vinegar in a small bowl and mix until the sugar dissolves. Add the oil in a fine stream, whisking until the mixture is well blended.

Friendship with oneself is all-important, because without it one
cannot be friends with anyone else in the world.

—*Eleanor Roosevelt*

Avocado Crab Cakes

These make a great change from chip-and-dip appetizers. Make a dazzling presentation by arranging the cakes with alternating slices of thinly sliced lemon and avocado.

1 pound blue crab meat
1 avocado
1/4 cup chopped green onions
1 egg, beaten

2 tablespoons fresh lemon juice
1 tablespoon prepared mustard (optional)
3/4 cup seasoned bread crumbs
1/4 cup olive oil

Place the crab meat in a large mixing bowl. Discard any shell and cartilage and flake the crab meat if necessary. Chop the avocado into small pieces. Add the avocado and green onions to the crab meat and toss to mix. Add the egg, lemon juice and mustard and mix well. Stir in 1/4 cup of the bread crumbs.

Shape the mixture into 6 cakes. Place the remaining 1/2 cup bread crumbs in a shallow dish. Place the crab cakes 1 at a time in the dish and shake gently to coat on both sides with the bread crumbs.

Heat the olive oil in a skillet over medium-high heat. Cook the crab cakes 3 at a time in the hot oil until golden brown on both sides, turning gently. Drain on paper towels and keep warm. Place on a serving plate.

YIELD: 3 SERVINGS

The best and most beautiful things in the world cannot be seen or even touched. They must be felt with the heart.

—Helen Keller

Ham and Cheese Roll-Ups

*The technique described for slicing the roll-ups will also work
for most bread and cake slicing.*

1 (6-ounce) can chopped ham
3 ounces cream cheese, softened
1/4 teaspoon garlic powder
2 tablespoons lemon juice

1 teaspoon dried minced onion
1 (8-count) can crescent rolls
1/4 cup sesame seeds

Drain the ham. Combine the ham, cream cheese, garlic powder, lemon juice and onion in a bowl and mix well. Separate the roll dough into 4 rectangles. Place the rectangles on a work surface and press the perforations to seal. Spread the ham mixture on the rectangles and roll each as for a jelly roll.

Cut a 12- to 14-inch length of quilting thread. Hold one end of the thread in each hand, slip the center of the thread under one end of a roll-up, cross the thread ends over the roll-up and pull until the thread makes a clean cut. Repeat, cutting each of the roll-ups into 6 or 7 slices. Coat the outer edge of each slice with the sesame seeds. Place the slices cut side down on an ungreased baking sheet. Bake at 325 to 350 degrees for 15 minutes or until golden brown. Serve warm or cool.

YIELD: 4 TO 6 SERVINGS

Mushroom Cheese Melts

1 pound fresh mushrooms
2 medium onions, chopped
2 tablespoons butter
1 to 2 loaves sliced cocktail pumpernickel
   or rye bread

3 cups shredded Swiss cheese
1 cup grated Parmesan cheese
1 cup (about) dry bread crumbs

Cut the mushrooms into thin slices. Sauté the mushrooms and onions in the butter in a large skillet until the onions are tender and the mushrooms are beginning to brown. Remove from the heat. Spread about 1 tablespoon of the mushroom mixture on each bread slice and arrange on a baking sheet. Sprinkle the slices generously with the Swiss cheese. Broil just until the cheese begins to melt. Remove from the broiler. Sprinkle generous amounts of the Parmesan cheese and the bread crumbs over the top. Broil for 1 to 2 minutes or until the cheese melts and the bread crumbs are brown. Serve immediately.

YIELD: 24 TO 30 SERVINGS

STUFFED MUSHROOMS

1 pound button mushrooms
1 onion, chopped
1/2 cup (1 stick) margarine

1 (6-ounce) can minced clams
1 stack butter crackers

Remove the stems from the mushrooms and chop finely. Sauté the chopped mushroom stems and onion in half the margarine in a medium skillet until the onion is tender. Remove from the heat. Add the undrained clams and mix well. Process the butter crackers in a food processor until crushed. Add to the clam mixture and mix well.

Sauté the mushroom caps in the remaining 1/4 cup margarine in a large skillet until tender. Drain the mushroom caps and fill with the clam mixture. Arrange on a serving platter and serve warm.

YIELD: 4 SERVINGS

HOT MUSHROOM TURNOVERS

8 ounces cream cheese, softened
1/2 cup (1 stick) margarine, softened
1 1/2 cups flour
8 ounces mushrooms, minced
1 large onion, minced
3 tablespoons margarine

1/4 cup sour cream
1 teaspoon salt
1/4 teaspoon thyme
2 tablespoons flour
1 egg, beaten

Combine the cream cheese and softened margarine in a mixing bowl and beat until well blended. Add the 1 1/2 cups flour and mix until smooth. Chill, covered, for 1 hour.

Sauté the mushrooms and onion in the 3 tablespoons margarine in a skillet until tender. Remove from the heat and mix in the sour cream, salt, thyme and 2 tablespoons flour. Roll the chilled dough to 1/8-inch thickness on a lightly floured surface. Cut with a biscuit cutter.

Place 1 teaspoon of the mushroom filling on each circle, fold the circle over to enclose the filling and press the edges together to seal. Brush the turnovers with the beaten egg and arrange on an ungreased baking sheet. Bake at 450 degrees for 12 to 14 minutes or until golden brown.

YIELD: 3 DOZEN

Olivada Crostini

2 (6- to 8-ounce) cans pitted
   black olives
3 tablespoons pine nuts
2 large garlic cloves

3 tablespoons olive oil
1 baguette
2 roasted red peppers
2 slices mozzarella cheese

Drain the olives and combine with the pine nuts and garlic in a food processor. Pulse until the mixture is chopped to the desired consistency. Add the olive oil and process for several seconds to mix well. Place the mixture in a container and chill, covered, in the refrigerator. The mixture may be prepared up to 1 week ahead.

Slice the bread into 1-inch-thick slices and arrange on a baking sheet. Bake at 350 degrees for 10 minutes or until toasted. Cut the roasted red peppers into 2-inch strips and the cheese into 1-inch strips. Spread the olive paste on the bread, add the roasted pepper and cheese strips and garnish with a parsley sprig.

YIELD: 6 TO 8 SERVINGS

Party Pinwheels

The colors are particularly festive for the holidays.

16 ounces cream cheese, softened
1 (.4-ounce) envelope ranch salad
   dressing mix
1/2 cup minced red bell pepper

1/2 cup sliced green onions
1/4 cup sliced stuffed olives
3 to 4 (10-inch) flour tortillas

Combine the cream cheese and salad dressing mix in a mixing bowl and beat until smooth. Add the red pepper, green onions and olives and mix well. Spread about 3/4 cup of the mixture on each tortilla and roll up tightly as for a jelly roll.

Wrap the roll-ups individually in plastic wrap and refrigerate for 2 hours or longer. Cut the roll-ups into 1/2-inch slices and arrange on a serving plate. Refrigerate any leftovers.

YIELD: 15 TO 20 SERVINGS

Liver Sausage Party Breads

8 ounces liver sausage
1 tablespoon minced onion
1 garlic clove, minced
1/4 teaspoon sage
1/4 teaspoon salt
2 tablespoons minced parsley

24 slices party rye bread
3 tablespoons (about) butter, softened
3 tablespoons (about) prepared mustard
6 stuffed olives, sliced

Combine the liver sausage, onion, garlic, sage, salt and parsley in a mixing bowl and beat with an electric mixer until well mixed. Spread the rye bread slices with a small amount of softened butter and then a small amount of mustard. Cover the slices with the liver sausage mixture. Arrange the slices on a baking sheet or broiler pan. Add slices of olive as garnish. Broil until light brown. Serve hot.

YIELD: 24 SERVINGS

Veggie Squares

Turn this recipe into your own creation by using your own combination of vegetables.

2 (8-count) packages crescent
  roll dough
16 ounces cream cheese, softened
1/2 cup mayonnaise
1/2 cup sour cream
1 (1-ounce) envelope ranch salad dressing
  mix

1 bunch broccoli
1/2 head cauliflower
1 bunch green onions
8 Roma tomatoes
1 cup finely shredded Cheddar cheese
1 cup finely shredded Monterey
  Jack cheese

Open the roll dough and separate into rectangles. Arrange the rectangles on a baking sheet to form one large rectangle, pressing the edges and perforations to seal. Bake at 350 degrees for 8 to 10 minutes or until golden brown. Let stand until completely cooled.

Combine the cream cheese, mayonnaise and sour cream in a mixing bowl and beat until smooth and creamy. Add the salad dressing mix and beat until well blended. Spread the mixture over the cooled crust.

Cut the broccoli and cauliflower into small pieces, slice the green onions and seed and chop the tomatoes. Layer the vegetables over the cream cheese mixture and sprinkle with the cheeses. Cover with plastic wrap. Refrigerate for 4 hours to overnight. Cut into squares.

YIELD: 4 DOZEN

Spinach Nuggets

2 (10-ounce) packages frozen chopped
   spinach
1 tablespoon dried minced onion
2 cups herb-seasoned stuffing croutons

1 cup grated Parmesan cheese
2 eggs, beaten
3 tablespoons melted butter or margarine

Cook the spinach with the dried onion according to the spinach package directions and drain well. Place the spinach mixture in a mixing bowl. Add the croutons and cheese and mix well. Add the eggs and melted butter and mix well. Shape the mixture into 1-inch balls and arrange in a shallow 9×13-inch baking pan. Bake at 375 degrees for 15 to 20 minutes or until firm and light brown.

YIELD: 4 DOZEN

Gazpacho

2 tomatoes
1/2 zucchini
1/2 summer squash
1/4 teaspoon minced onion
1/4 teaspoon minced garlic
1/2 cup thick and chunky salsa

3 tablespoons balsamic vinaigrette
   dressing
1 (48-ounce) can vegetable juice cocktail
Coarsely ground black pepper to taste
Croutons

Seed and chop the tomatoes and place in a large bowl or pitcher. Peel and chop the zucchini and summer squash and add to the tomatoes. Add the onion, garlic, salsa, vinaigrette dressing and vegetable juice cocktail. Add the pepper and mix well. Refrigerate, covered, for several hours. Pour into soup cups and garnish with parsley sprigs. Serve with the Croutons.

YIELD: 6 SERVINGS

Croutons

Olive oil
2 cups bread cubes

Italian seasoning to taste

Pour enough olive oil into a large skillet to just coat the bottom of the skillet. Heat over medium-high heat. Add the bread cubes. Toast over medium heat until brown and crisp on all sides, tossing frequently. Sprinkle with Italian seasoning and additional olive oil, tossing gently to coat.

BUTTERNUT SQUASH SOUP

Serve this soup as a lovely beginning to a Thanksgiving or Christmas dinner.

1 large butternut squash	2 cups chicken broth
1 onion, chopped	1 cup heavy cream
2 tablespoons butter	Salt and pepper to taste

Peel the squash and cut into cubes. Sauté the onion in the butter in a large saucepan until tender. Add the chicken broth and mix well. Bring the mixture to a simmer. Add the squash. Simmer until the squash is tender. Process the squash mixture in a blender or food processor until smooth. Return to the saucepan and blend in the cream. Heat to serving temperature but do not boil. Season with salt and pepper. Ladle into soup bowls.

YIELD: 4 TO 6 SERVINGS

CURRIED ZUCCHINI SOUP

Prepare this delicious soup while zucchini is fresh from the garden and freeze to enjoy later. Just pour the puréed mixture into freezer containers for storage, thaw at room temperature and add the cream, salt and pepper. Then chill or heat as desired.

2¹/₂ pounds zucchini	2 cups chicken stock
2 large yellow onions	2 cups light cream
3 tablespoons butter	Salt and pepper to taste
1 tablespoon (or more) curry powder	

Cut the zucchini and onions into thin slices. Sauté the zucchini and onions in the butter in a large skillet until tender. Add the curry powder and cook until the vegetables are very tender, stirring occasionally. Add the chicken stock. Simmer, covered, for 10 minutes. Purée the mixture in a blender or food processor. Pour into a saucepan. Blend in the cream and add the salt and pepper.

Heat to serving temperature over low heat to serve hot. Serve cold by blending in the cream, salt and pepper and chilling for 6 hours or longer.

YIELD: 4 SERVINGS

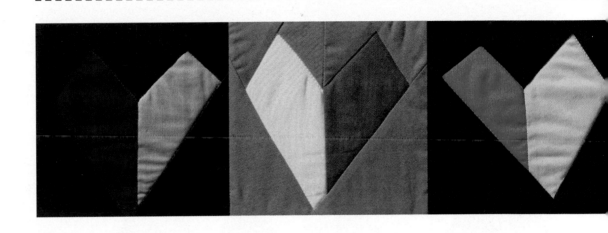

HEARTY SALADS
AND SOUPS

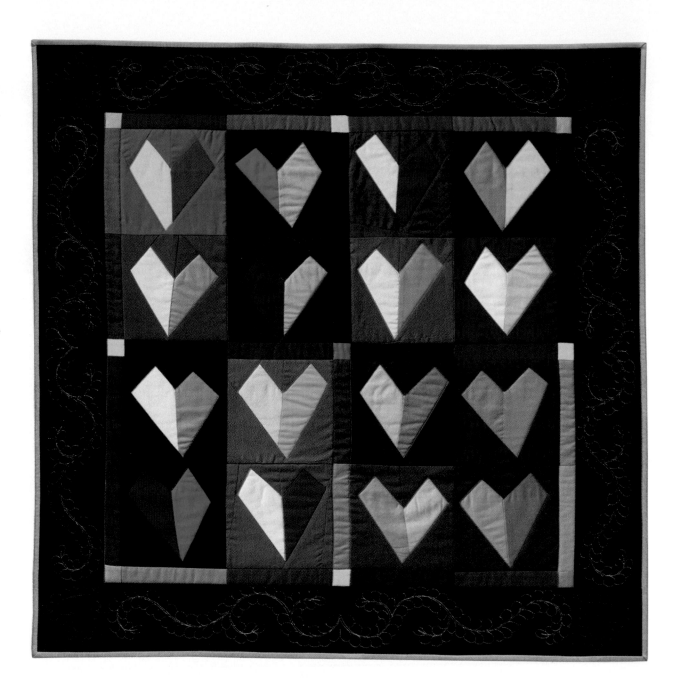

Simply Hearts Quilt
34" × 34"

The Amish are a simple, humble people devoted to family, religion, and community. For many generations they have created quilts that have come to be valued as pieces of abstract art. But designing pieces of art was the furthest thing from the minds of the Amish women who made these extraordinary solid-color quilts, especially those made between the late 1800s and the 1940s, to cover beds and to keep their families warm.

Coming to America from Europe in search of religious freedom during the eighteenth century, the Amish established a strong community life known for its simplicity, austerity, and rejection of worldly ways. They borrowed the tradition of quilting from their "English" neighbors and interpreted it in a unique way, developing patterns and distinctive color schemes that were their own. In keeping with their belief that anything worth doing is worth doing well, they stitched ornate hand-quilted patterns across the surface of their bold, geometric designs. The Amish women used their innate, uninhibited sense of color and design to create functional bed coverings that just happened to be works of art.

SOUTHWEST CORN AND BEAN SALAD

1 (15-ounce) can black beans
1 (8-ounce) can whole kernel corn
1 (2-ounce) can sliced black olives
1 (4-ounce) can chopped green chiles
 (optional)
4 ounces Monterey Jack cheese
3/4 cup thinly sliced celery
1/4 cup sliced green onions with tops

1 small red bell pepper, chopped, or
 4 ounces chopped pimentos
3/4 cup picante sauce
2 tablespoons lemon juice
2 tablespoons olive oil
1/2 to 1 teaspoon ground cumin
1 garlic clove, minced

Drain the black beans, rinse with cool water and drain well. Drain the corn, olives and green chiles and combine with the beans in a large bowl. Cut the cheese into 1/4-inch cubes and add to the bowl. Add the celery, green onions, red pepper, picante sauce, lemon juice, olive oil, cumin and garlic and mix well. Refrigerate, covered, for several hours to overnight. Serve with tortilla chips.

YIELD: 8 SERVINGS

CONFETTI CORN SALAD

2 (12-ounce) cans whole kernel corn,
 drained
3 pounds fresh tomatoes, chopped, or
 2 (16-ounce) cans diced tomatoes
4 large green bell peppers, chopped
4 medium onions, chopped
1/2 cup vinegar

1/2 cup vegetable oil
2 teaspoons salt
2 teaspoons pepper
2 teaspoons dry mustard
1 tablespoon celery seeds, or
 1 cup chopped celery
Sugar to taste

Combine the corn, tomatoes, green peppers and onions in a large bowl. Combine the vinegar, oil, salt, pepper, dry mustard, celery seeds and sugar in a small bowl and mix well. Pour over the vegetable mixture and mix gently. Refrigerate, covered, for several hours before serving.

YIELD: 8 TO 10 SERVINGS

The world is round so that friendship may encircle it.

Italian Bread Salad

Serve this salad in small portions as a side dish or enjoy heartier
servings as a healthy main dish.

1/2 loaf Italian bread
Nonstick cooking spray
1/4 cup olive oil
2 tablespoons balsamic vinegar
1/4 teaspoon salt

1/4 teaspoon pepper
2 large tomatoes
1 large cucumber
1 medium red onion
1 (15-ounce) can cannellini beans

Cut the bread into cubes of the desired size for croutons. Place the bread cubes in a large bowl. Spray generously with the cooking spray, toss to mix and repeat the spraying and tossing. Spread the prepared bread cubes on a baking sheet. Bake at 375 degrees for 8 to 10 minutes or until golden brown and set aside to cool.

Combine the olive oil, vinegar, salt and pepper in a large bowl. Cut the tomatoes, cucumber and red onion into pieces of the desired size. Drain, rinse and drain the beans. Add the tomatoes, cucumber, onion and beans to the olive oil mixture and toss until coated. Add the toasted bread cubes, toss gently and serve immediately.

YIELD: 6 SERVINGS

Greek Salad

Salads that "travel" well to carry to potlucks and picnics are
rarely as tasty and attractive as this one.

1 (10-ounce) package fresh spinach
1 (8-ounce) bottle oil and vinegar
  Greek salad dressing
1/2 small red onion, coarsely chopped

6 kalamata olives, pitted, quartered
1 small red bell pepper, chopped
Feta cheese to taste, crumbled
4 slices bacon, crisp-cooked, crumbled

Rinse the spinach well, drain, pat dry and discard the tough stems. Tear the leaves into small pieces. Heat a large saucepan or skillet over low heat. Add the spinach. Cook just until the spinach begins to wilt, tossing constantly. Place the pan in a larger pan of cold water to stop the cooking. Sprinkle a few drops of the salad dressing at a time over the spinach, tossing constantly until the spinach is coated with the desired amount of the dressing. Add the onion and olives and toss to mix. Place the spinach mixture in a salad bowl. Sprinkle the red pepper, feta cheese and bacon over the top. Chill, covered, until serving time.

YIELD: 4 SERVINGS

Pizza Pasta Salad

1 pound spiral macaroni
3 medium tomatoes, seeded, chopped
3 cups shredded Cheddar cheese
1 to 2 bunches green onions, sliced
3 ounces pepperoni, thinly sliced
3/4 cup vegetable oil
2/3 cup grated Parmesan cheese

1/2 cup red wine vinegar
2 teaspoons dried oregano or Italian
  seasoning
1 teaspoon garlic powder
1/2 teaspoon salt
1/4 teaspoon pepper
Croutons (optional)

Cook the macaroni according to the package directions, drain, rinse with cold water and drain well. Combine the macaroni, tomatoes, Cheddar cheese, green onions and pepperoni in a large bowl and toss to mix.

Combine the oil, Parmesan cheese, vinegar, oregano, garlic powder, salt and pepper in a small bowl and mix well. Pour over the macaroni mixture and mix gently. Refrigerate, covered, for several hours. Toss the salad and top with croutons just before serving.

YIELD: 16 TO 20 SERVINGS

Tabbouleh

*Be sure to prepare this salad at least a day ahead so
the flavors have time to develop.*

3/4 cup bulgur wheat
4 firm tomatoes, peeled, chopped
3 scallions, finely chopped
6 tablespoons fresh lemon juice

5 tablespoons extra-virgin olive oil
6 tablespoons chopped fresh parsley
1/4 cup chopped fresh mint
Salt and pepper to taste

Place the bulgur in a bowl. Cover with cold water and let stand for 20 minutes. Drain well and squeeze out excess water. Place the bulgur in a bowl and add the tomatoes and scallions. Combine the lemon juice, olive oil, parsley, mint, salt and pepper in a small bowl and mix well. Pour over the bulgur mixture and mix well. Refrigerate, covered, for several hours to overnight.

YIELD: 4 SERVINGS

Taco Salad

2 pounds ground beef
1 medium onion
2 heads lettuce
4 medium tomatoes

4 cups shredded Cheddar cheese
1 large package spicy nacho chips
1 (16-ounce) bottle French salad dressing

Brown the ground beef in a large skillet, stirring until crumbly and drain well. Chop the onion, lettuce and tomatoes into desired size pieces. Combine the chopped vegetables, ground beef and cheese in a large salad bowl and toss to mix. Crush the spicy nacho chips in the package to the desired coarseness and add to the salad. Add the desired amount of salad dressing and toss to mix. Serve immediately.

YIELD: 25 SERVINGS

Pasta Taco Salad

1 pound ground beef
1/2 cup chopped onion
2 envelopes taco seasoning mix
1 pound fettuccini
1 (16-ounce) can kidney beans
1 (16-ounce) can black beans
1 (4-ounce) can chopped green chiles, drained
1 (16-ounce) can pitted black olives, drained, sliced

2 cups thinly sliced celery
1 1/2 cups shredded Cheddar cheese
3 tomatoes, seeded, chopped
2 bunches green onions, sliced
1 cup mild salsa
2 1/4 cups Catalina salad dressing
1 large package tortilla chips

Brown the ground beef with the onion in a large skillet, stirring until the ground beef is crumbly and drain well. Stir in the taco seasoning mix and set aside. Cook the fettuccini according to the package directions, drain, rinse with cold water and drain well. Drain the canned beans, rinse and drain well.

Combine the fettuccini, ground beef mixture, beans, green chiles, olives, celery, cheese, tomatoes and green onions in a large bowl and toss to mix. Add the salsa and salad dressing and toss well. Refrigerate, covered, for several hours to allow flavors to marry. Serve with tortilla chips.

YIELD: 20 TO 25 SERVINGS

Blackened Chicken Caesar Salad

Serve this salad with buttered sourdough rolls and your favorite white wine.

1/4 cup olive oil
1 garlic clove, minced
4 teaspoons fresh lemon juice
1/2 teaspoon Worcestershire sauce
1/4 teaspoon finely ground pepper
4 boneless skinless chicken breasts

1 (3-ounce) bottle Cajun seasoning
3 tablespoons vegetable oil
8 cups torn romaine
1 cup croutons
Freshly shredded Parmesan cheese to taste

For the dressing, combine the first 5 ingredients in a small jar, shake vigorously and chill in the refrigerator. Pound the chicken breasts to 1/4-inch thickness between waxed paper. Coat the chicken lightly on all sides with the Cajun seasoning. Heat the vegetable oil in a large heavy skillet until very hot. Add the chicken and cook for several minutes on each side until the juices run clear; set aside. Divide the romaine among 4 plates. Drizzle the desired amount of chilled dressing over the romaine, add the croutons and a generous amount of the Parmesan cheese. Slice the chicken into strips and arrange on the salads.

YIELD: 4 SERVINGS

Chinese Chicken Noodle Salad

What more could you ask for—easy, speedy, make-ahead, well-balanced, and low-fat.
Make it in the morning and then quilt until dinnertime.

4 ounces angel hair pasta
1 cup (1-inch pieces) green vegetable,
    such as asparagus, green beans,
    broccoli or snow peas
2 cups shredded cooked chicken
1/2 cup chopped red bell pepper
1/4 cup sliced green onions

1 medium cucumber, peeled, chopped
3 tablespoons soy sauce
2 tablespoons seasoned rice vinegar
2 teaspoons sesame seeds, toasted
1 teaspoon dark sesame oil
1/4 teaspoon pepper

Break the pasta into 5-inch lengths. Bring a pot of water to a boil. Add the pasta and cook for 2 minutes. Add the vegetable pieces, return the water to a boil and cook for 1 minute. Drain, rinse with cold water and drain well. Combine the pasta mixture, chicken, red pepper, green onions and cucumber in a large bowl and toss to mix. Combine the soy sauce, rice vinegar, sesame seeds, sesame oil and pepper in a small bowl and mix well. Add to the pasta mixture and toss to mix. Refrigerate, covered, until serving time.

YIELD: 4 SERVINGS

Ginger Chicken Salad

Healthy and quick to prepare in advance. It will taste as though you've spent hours in the kitchen. Serve the salad on lettuce-lined plates with crispy bread.

1¹/₂ pounds cooked boned chicken
4 ribs celery, sliced
6 green onions, sliced
8 ounces white seedless grapes, cut into halves

4 to 6 ounces crystallized ginger, finely chopped
4 ounces walnut pieces
1 cup low-fat mayonnaise
1 cup low-fat plain yogurt

Cut the chicken into desired size pieces and place in a large bowl. Add the celery, green onions, grapes, ginger and walnuts and toss to mix. Blend the mayonnaise and yogurt in a small bowl. Add to the salad and toss to mix. Refrigerate, covered, for 3 hours or longer.

YIELD: 4 SERVINGS

Quilters' Chicken Salad

6 to 8 boneless skinless chicken breasts
4 teaspoons sesame oil
2 tablespoons soy sauce
¹/₄ teaspoon salt
1 teaspoon sugar
Mrs. Dash or garlic and herbs to taste
2 to 3 cups broccoli florets
2 to 3 cups red seedless grapes
2 to 3 cups green seedless grapes

1 cup golden raisins
1 cup dried cranberries
1 cup coarsely chopped pecans
¹/₂ cup nonfat mayonnaise-type salad dressing
¹/₂ cup nonfat mayonnaise
3 tablespoons vinegar
¹/₃ to ¹/₂ cup sugar

Cut the chicken into 1-inch pieces and place in a bowl. Combine the sesame oil, soy sauce, salt, sugar and Mrs. Dash in a small bowl and mix well. Pour over the chicken pieces, stirring to coat. Marinate the chicken, covered, in the refrigerator overnight, stirring occasionally. Drain the chicken and discard the marinade.

Preheat a heavy skillet or wok over medium-high heat. Add the chicken and stir-fry until the juices run clear. Drain the chicken and chill in the refrigerator. Rinse the broccoli and grapes, pat dry and place in a large bowl. Add the raisins, cranberries and pecans and toss to mix. Combine the salad dressing, mayonnaise, vinegar and sugar in a small bowl and blend well. Add to the broccoli mixture and toss lightly to mix. Add the chicken and toss lightly. Refrigerate, covered, until serving time.

YIELD: 12 SERVINGS

ATHENIAN SALAD WITH GRILLED PORK

Prepare Homemade Greek Vinaigrette by whisking together 1/3 cup olive oil, the juice of 1 1/2 lemons, 2 teaspoons dried oregano, 1/4 cup chopped fresh parsley and salt and pepper to taste. Serve this delicious salad with warm pita bread and papaya halves.

1 (1-pound) pork tenderloin, butterflied
3/4 cup bottled or Homemade Greek Vinaigrette (see Headnote)
1/4 cup chopped fresh parsley (optional)
1 (10-ounce) package salad greens

1/2 cup crumbled feta cheese
Black olives
1 tomato, chopped (optional)
1 cucumber, peeled, seeded, chopped (optional)
Salt and pepper to taste

Place the pork in a sealable plastic bag and add half the vinaigrette and the parsley. Squeeze the air from the bag and seal tightly. Marinate the pork in the refrigerator for about 20 minutes while preheating the grill.

Drain the pork and discard the marinade. Place the pork on the grill. Cook for 10 to 12 minutes or to 155 degrees on a meat thermometer. Let the pork stand for 5 minutes before slicing. Spread the salad greens on a platter. Add the pork slices, feta cheese, olives, tomato and cucumber. Sprinkle with salt and pepper and drizzle the remaining vinaigrette over the top.

YIELD: 4 SERVINGS

GOLDEN PAPAYA AND CRAB SALAD

1 pound cooked crab meat
8 ounces sugar snap peas
1/2 small red onion, chopped
2 medium papayas, chopped
4 ounces mesclun
1/2 head leafy lettuce, torn

1/4 cup fresh lime juice
2 tablespoons olive oil
2 dashes of Tabasco sauce
1 teaspoon sugar
Salt and pepper to taste
1/4 cup chopped fresh parsley

Flake or chop the crab meat as desired and place in a bowl. Add the peas, onion, papayas, mesclun and lettuce and toss to mix. Combine the lime juice, olive oil, Tabasco sauce, sugar, salt, pepper and parsley in a small bowl and mix well. Pour over the salad and toss lightly. Serve immediately.

YIELD: 4 SERVINGS

ARTICHOKE AND SHRIMP SALAD

Serve with warm crusty bread for a delightful summer lunch.

1 (14-ounce) can artichoke hearts
1 pound frozen cooked peeled medium or
  large shrimp
1 cup pitted black olives

1 (16-ounce) bottle Italian salad dressing
  with oil
1 cup cherry tomato halves

Drain the artichoke hearts and cut into quarters. Thaw the shrimp, rinse and pat dry. Combine the artichoke hearts, shrimp and olives in a large sealable plastic bag. Add the salad dressing, squeeze out most of the air and seal the bag. Marinate the salad in the refrigerator overnight, turning the bag occasionally.

Drain the salad and discard the dressing. Place the shrimp mixture in a salad bowl, add the cherry tomatoes and toss lightly. Garnish with sprigs of fresh herbs and nasturtium blossoms.

YIELD: 8 SERVINGS

OVERNIGHT VEGETABLE SALAD

Toss the salad before serving or, for a spectacular effect, leave the layers intact and serve by scooping through all the layers with large salad tongs.

1 head lettuce, torn
Sugar, salt and pepper to taste
1 (7-ounce) can sliced water chestnuts,
  drained
1 (10-ounce) package frozen peas, thawed,
  drained

1 cup chopped celery
$1/2$ cup chopped onion
1 pound bacon, crisp-cooked, crumbled
4 medium tomatoes, chopped, drained
2 cups shredded Swiss cheese
1 cup mayonnaise

Line the bottom of a large glass bowl with about 3 cups of the lettuce and sprinkle with sugar, salt and pepper. Layer the water chestnuts, peas, celery, onion, bacon, remaining lettuce, tomatoes and Swiss cheese over the top.

Spread the mayonnaise over the cheese, sealing to the edge of the bowl. Refrigerate, covered, overnight or for up to 24 hours. Garnish with sliced green onions and paprika.

YIELD: 12 TO 15 SERVINGS

FARMERS' MARKET SOUR CREAM DRESSING

1 cup sour cream
1 garlic clove, minced
2 tablespoons minced green onions
1 teaspoon lemon juice

1/4 cup red wine vinegar
3 tablespoons minced fresh parsley
3 ounces bleu cheese, crumbled

Combine the sour cream, garlic, green onions, lemon juice and vinegar in a small bowl and mix well. Stir in the parsley and bleu cheese. Store in an airtight container in the refrigerator.

YIELD: 1½ CUPS

POPPY SEED SALAD DRESSING

Use this dressing on a salad of spinach with sliced strawberries and sliced almonds. Add the dressing at the last minute.

1½ cups sugar
2 teaspoons dry mustard
1 teaspoon salt

2/3 cup apple cider
1⅓ cups vegetable oil
3 tablespoons poppy seeds

Combine the sugar, dry mustard and salt in a small bowl. Add the cider and oil and mix well. Let the mixture stand at room temperature, stirring frequently until the sugar dissolves. Stir in the poppy seeds. Store in an airtight container in the refrigerator.

YIELD: 2½ CUPS

SWEET-AND-SOUR SALAD DRESSING

Sugar substitute equivalent to the amount of sugar listed may be used with no change in flavor.

1/2 cup olive oil
1/4 cup cider vinegar
1/4 cup sugar
1/2 teaspoon salt
1/2 teaspoon paprika

1/4 teaspoon dry mustard
1/4 teaspoon celery salt
1 tablespoon minced onion
6 grinds of pepper

Combine the olive oil, vinegar, sugar and salt in small jar and shake until the sugar and salt dissolve. Add the remaining ingredients and shake vigorously to mix. Store in the refrigerator.

YIELD: 1 CUP

Autumn Soup

This is a very forgiving recipe: you can use broth instead of water or double any of the vegetables or make many other variations to your taste. It always comes out perfect.

1 pound ground beef
1 cup chopped onion
1 cup chopped peeled potatoes
1 cup chopped carrots
1 cup chopped celery

2 teaspoons garlic powder
Red pepper flakes to taste
Salt and black pepper to taste
2 (16-ounce) cans stewed tomatoes

Brown the ground beef with the onion in a soup pot, stirring until the ground beef is crumbly and drain. Add the potatoes, carrots, celery, garlic powder, red pepper flakes, salt and black pepper and enough water to just cover, mixing well. Simmer for 20 minutes. Add the tomatoes and simmer for 10 minutes longer. Add additional tomatoes or water to make the soup of the desired consistency. Serve immediately.

YIELD: 4 SERVINGS

Beef Minestrone

1 pound ground round
1 cup chopped onion
1 cup chopped peeled potatoes
1 cup chopped tomatoes
1 cup shredded cabbage
$1/2$ cup chopped celery

$1/4$ cup uncooked long grain rice
$1/2$ teaspoon each dried basil and thyme
$1/4$ teaspoon pepper
1 bay leaf
6 cups water
5 teaspoons grated Parmesan cheese

Brown the ground beef with the onion in a Dutch oven, stirring until the ground beef is crumbly and drain well. Add the potatoes, tomatoes, cabbage, celery, rice, basil, thyme, pepper, bay leaf and water and mix well. Bring to a boil, reduce the heat and simmer, covered, for 1 hour. Discard the bay leaf. Ladle into soup bowls and sprinkle each serving with $1/2$ teaspoon of the cheese.

YIELD: 10 SERVINGS

Plant kindness, gather love.

HAMBURGER SOUP

1 pound lean ground beef
3 medium carrots, thinly sliced
1 large onion, chopped
4 ribs celery, thinly sliced
1 (15-ounce) can Great Northern beans
1 (8-ounce) can lima beans
1 (15-ounce) can whole kernel corn

1 (16-ounce) can stewed tomatoes
1/2 cup barley
4 beef bouillon cubes
5 cups water
2 teaspoons chili powder
Salt to taste

Brown the ground beef in a skillet, stirring until crumbly and drain well. Place the ground beef in a slow cooker. Add the carrots, onion, celery, undrained beans, corn, tomatoes and barley and mix well. Dissolve the bouillon cubes in the water and stir into the cooker with the chili powder and salt. Cook on Low for 8 to 10 hours. Experiment with adding your family's favorite ingredients—leftover green beans are especially good.

YIELD: 6 TO 8 SERVINGS

NEW ENGLAND CLAM CHOWDER

3 (6-ounce) cans chopped clams
3 slices thick bacon, chopped
4 or 5 medium russet potatoes, peeled, chopped
1 cup chopped onion
3 or 4 ribs celery, chopped
1/2 teaspoon salt

1/2 cup (1 stick) margarine
3/4 cup flour
2 cups half-and-half
2 cups milk
1/2 teaspoon garlic salt
Pepper to taste

Drain the clams, reserving the liquid. Brown the bacon in a heavy saucepan or stockpot over medium to high heat. Stir in the potatoes, onion, celery and salt. Sauté over medium-high heat for 5 minutes. Add the reserved clam liquid and just enough water to cover the vegetables and mix well. Simmer, covered, for 10 to 12 minutes or until the potatoes and celery are tender, stirring occasionally. Heat the margarine in a saucepan over medium heat until melted. Whisk in the flour until smooth. Add the half-and-half and milk gradually, whisking constantly. Cook over low heat until thickened, stirring constantly. Stir in the clams and garlic salt. Add the clam mixture to the potato mixture and mix gently. Cook over low heat for 5 minutes or until heated through, stirring occasionally. Season with pepper. Ladle into soup bowls.

YIELD: 6 TO 8 SERVINGS

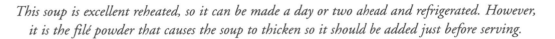

HOOSIER CHICKEN GUMBO

This soup is excellent reheated, so it can be made a day or two ahead and refrigerated. However, it is the filé powder that causes the soup to thicken so it should be added just before serving.

2 tablespoons vegetable oil
2 tablespoons flour
2 slices bacon, chopped
1¼ cups coarsely chopped onion
2 garlic cloves, chopped
²/3 cup chopped green bell pepper
1 teaspoon salt
1 teaspoon coarsely ground pepper

2 teaspoons Worcestershire sauce
1 teaspoon hot pepper sauce
4 cups stewed tomatoes
3 pounds chicken breasts
4 cups water
1 (10-ounce) package frozen sliced okra
2 teaspoons filé powder (optional)
Hot cooked rice

Mix the oil and flour in a Dutch oven over medium heat. Cook until the flour is golden brown, stirring constantly. Add the bacon to the roux and cook until brown, stirring frequently. Add the onion, garlic and green pepper and cook for 4 to 5 minutes, stirring frequently. Add the salt, pepper, Worcestershire sauce, hot pepper sauce and tomatoes and mix well. Add the chicken and water. Bring the mixture to a boil and reduce the heat. Simmer, covered, for 45 minutes or until the chicken is tender. Remove the chicken from the soup. Discard the skin and bones and cut the chicken into bite-size pieces. Skim the soup, return to a boil, add the okra and reduce the heat to a simmer. Simmer for 15 minutes, stirring occasionally. Add the chicken and filé powder and mix well. Heat to serving temperature. Serve in soup bowls over hot cooked rice.

YIELD: 10 SERVINGS

CANADELI

12 ounces bacon, minced
4 ounces hard salami, minced
¼ cup chopped fresh parsley
8 cups low-sodium chicken broth

1 (1-pound) loaf white bread
2 cups milk
4 eggs, beaten
2 cups (about) flour

Cook the bacon, salami and parsley in a large skillet until brown and crisp. Drain and set aside. Heat the broth in a soup pot over medium heat. Cut the bread into small cubes and place in a large bowl. Add the milk and eggs and mix well. Add enough flour gradually to make a stiff dough. Mix in the bacon mixture. Bring the broth to a boil. Drop the dough by spoonfuls into the hot broth, dipping the spoon into the broth each time. Reduce the heat to a simmer. Simmer, covered, for 45 minutes.

YIELD: 6 SERVINGS

ITALIAN CHICKEN AND SAUSAGE SOUP

3 or 4 sweet or hot Italian sausages
2 to 3 cups water
4 boneless skinless chicken breasts
1 medium onion, chopped
2 garlic cloves, minced
2 ribs celery, chopped
1 small red or green bell pepper, chopped
4 ounces fresh mushrooms, sliced
2 to 3 tablespoons olive oil

6 to 8 cups chicken stock
3 or 4 Italian plum tomatoes, chopped
3 to 4 tablespoons Italian herb seasoning
2 tablespoons tomato paste
1 (16-ounce) can cannellini beans,
   drained
$1/4$ cup ditalini
Salt and pepper to taste
Freshly grated Parmesan cheese

Parboil the sausages in the water in a saucepan for 5 to 7 minutes. Drain, slice the sausage into $1/2$-inch pieces and set aside. Cut the chicken into small pieces and set aside. Sauté the onion, garlic, celery, bell pepper and mushrooms in the olive oil in a 6-quart soup pot until the vegetables are tender. Add the chicken stock, sausage, chicken, tomatoes, seasoning and tomato paste and mix well. Bring to a boil, stirring occasionally. Reduce the heat to a simmer. Simmer, covered, for $13/4$ hours. Add the beans and/or the pasta. Cook for 15 minutes or just until the pasta is tender. Ladle the soup into bowls, season with salt and pepper and sprinkle with Parmesan cheese.

YIELD: 10 TO 12 SERVINGS

BARLEY AND MUSHROOM SOUP

1 cup quick-cooking pearl barley, or
   $1/2$ cup pearl barley
7 cups chicken stock or water
3 onions, chopped
4 carrots, chopped
2 ribs celery, chopped

2 cups chopped fresh mushrooms
$1/2$ cup (1 stick) butter
2 teaspoons salt
1 teaspoon pepper
1 to $11/2$ cups sour cream

Combine the barley and half the chicken stock in a medium saucepan and simmer for 1 hour. Combine the onions, carrots, celery and mushrooms in a soup pot. Add the remaining chicken stock and simmer until the vegetables are tender. Add the barley mixture, butter, salt and pepper to the vegetable mixture and mix well. Remove from the heat and mix in the sour cream. Garnish the servings with chopped parsley. Serve hot or cold.

YIELD: 8 SERVINGS

Onion Soup

1 tablespoon butter
2 medium onions, thinly sliced
1/4 teaspoon sugar
1 teaspoon flour

1 (10-ounce) can beef broth
4 slices French bread
1/2 to 1 cup shredded mozzarella or
    Swiss cheese

Melt the butter in a heavy skillet over low heat. Add the onions and cook over low heat for 1 hour or until golden brown, stirring frequently. Add the sugar and flour and cook for 2 to 3 minutes, stirring constantly. Add the broth and 1 soup can water. Simmer, loosely covered, for 30 minutes. May prepare ahead up to this point.

Ladle the soup into 4 ovenproof soup bowls. Place the bowls on a baking sheet. Float a bread slice on each bowl and cover the bread with the cheese. Bake at 400 degrees for about 10 minutes or until the cheese is melted.

YIELD: 4 SERVINGS

Potato Soup

1/3 cup chopped celery
1/3 cup chopped onion
1 carrot, finely grated
3 cups chopped peeled potatoes
2 chicken bouillon cubes

1 cup milk
1 tablespoon flour
3 ounces cream cheese
Salt and pepper to taste

Combine the celery, onion and carrot in a large saucepan. Add a small amount of water and simmer until the vegetables are tender. Add the potatoes, bouillon cubes and enough water to cover. Simmer until the potatoes are tender, stirring occasionally.

Mix the milk with the flour. Add the milk mixture to the soup and cook until the soup is thickened, stirring frequently. Cut the cream cheese into small pieces and stir into the soup until the cream cheese melts. Season with salt and pepper.

YIELD: 5 SERVINGS

There is nothing like staying at home for real comfort.

—*Jane Austen*

Hearty Spinach and Mushroom Soup

8 ounces fresh mushrooms, sliced
1/2 cup chopped onion
1/2 cup shredded carrots
2 teaspoons margarine or vegetable oil
1 (14-ounce) can chicken broth
1 (10-ounce) package frozen chopped
  spinach, thawed, drained

1/8 teaspoon nutmeg
Pepper to taste
2 cups milk
1/4 cup flour
4 ounces low-fat cream cheese
1 cup shredded Cheddar cheese

Sauté the mushrooms, onion and carrots in the margarine in a skillet for 3 minutes. Add the chicken broth, spinach, nutmeg and pepper, mix well and remove from the heat. Whisk the milk and flour together in a 2-quart saucepan over low heat. Add the spinach mixture. Cook until thickened and bubbly, stirring constantly. Reduce the heat. Cut the cream cheese into small pieces and add the cream cheese and Cheddar cheese to the soup, stirring until the cheese melts. Serve the soup with French bread.

YIELD: 6 SERVINGS

Tortellini Soup

*This is a quick version of an old-fashioned soup. For a more
traditional soup, add small meatballs.*

1 onion, chopped
1 garlic clove, minced
3 carrots, chopped
5 plum tomatoes, chopped
3 tablespoons olive oil
2 small zucchini, chopped

Freshly ground pepper to taste
3 (14-ounce) cans low-fat chicken broth
1 package cheese tortellini
1 bunch escarole, chopped
Freshly grated Parmesan cheese

Sauté the onion, garlic, carrots and tomatoes in the olive oil in a large soup pot for 10 minutes. Add the zucchini, pepper and chicken broth and mix well. Bring to a simmer and simmer for 2 minutes. Add the tortellini and simmer for 4 minutes. Add the escarole and simmer for 4 minutes. Add the Parmesan cheese just before serving.

YIELD: 10 SERVINGS

MEAT ENTRÉES

Joyful Hearts Quilt
49" × 56"

The voices of women past and present can be heard through their quilts. Some speak in soft, gentle whispers or thoughtful, muted tones. Others make bold, witty statements. Emotions are expressed through pattern and color. Sweet pastel calicoes evoke images of romance and tradition; earth-toned plaids suggest home and family; and bold, vibrant stripes and polka dots shout with energy, excitement, and joy.

Quilts can calm the mind and soothe the soul; they can also light up a room and lift the spirit. A quilt has the powerful ability to change the way we feel through the language of color and texture, spoken through the needle, thread, personality, and artistry of the quiltmaker.

Sauerbraten with Potato Dumplings

1 (4-pound) bottom round or boneless
  chuck roast
2 teaspoons salt
1 teaspoon ground ginger
2 cups cider vinegar
2¹/2 cups water
2 medium onions, sliced
2 tablespoons mixed pickling spice

2 bay leaves
1 teaspoon black peppercorns
8 whole cloves
¹/3 cup sugar
2 tablespoons shortening
6 gingersnaps, crumbled
Potato Dumplings

Wipe the roast and rub all surfaces with a mixture of salt and ginger. Place the roast in a large bowl. Combine the vinegar, water, onions, pickling spice, bay leaves, peppercorns, cloves and sugar in a saucepan. Bring the mixture to a boil, stirring until the sugar dissolves. Pour the hot mixture over the roast. Let stand until cool. Marinate, covered, in the refrigerator for 3 days, turning the roast daily.

Remove the roast from the marinade. Reserve the marinade and wipe the roast with paper towels. Heat the shortening in a Dutch oven or other heavy kettle. Add the roast and brown on all sides. Place the roast on a rack in the Dutch oven. Add 1 cup of the reserved marinade and about half of the onion slices and spices from the marinade. Cover tightly and cook over very low heat for 3¹/2 hours or until very tender, adding small amounts of additional liquid as necessary.

Remove the roast to a platter. Strain the cooking liquid into a saucepan. Skim off and discard any excess fat. Strain in enough additional reserved marinade to measure about 2 cups liquid for the sauce. Bring the sauce to a simmer. Add the gingersnaps. Simmer until the sauce is thickened, stirring constantly. Slice the roast and serve with the Potato Dumplings and sauce. May omit the gingersnaps and thicken the cooking liquid with a small amount of flour blended with a small amount of cool water.

YIELD: 8 TO 10 SERVINGS

Potato Dumplings

8 medium potatoes
¹/2 cup sifted flour
1¹/2 teaspoons salt

2 eggs, lightly beaten
Salt to taste

Scrub the potatoes. Steam the unpeeled potatoes until tender. Cool, peel and force the potatoes through a potato ricer onto a large platter. Let the riced potatoes stand, uncovered, at room temperature overnight. Sprinkle the potatoes with the flour. Add 1¹/2 teaspoons salt and eggs and mix well. Shape into 8 to 10 balls. Bring a large kettle of salted water to a boil. Add the potato balls. Cook, uncovered, for 20 minutes. Drain and serve immediately.

California Barbecued Steak

1 (2¹/₂-pound) top sirloin or
   1 (2-pound) flank steak
³/₄ cup ketchup
³/₄ cup chili sauce
3 tablespoons honey
3 tablespoons hoisin sauce (optional)

3 tablespoons minced green onions
1¹/₂ tablespoons soy sauce
3 garlic cloves, minced
¹/₂ teaspoon salt
¹/₈ teaspoon pepper

Place the steak in a sealable plastic bag. (Score a flank steak diagonally on both sides before placing in the bag.) Combine the ketchup, chili sauce, honey, hoisin sauce, green onions, soy sauce, garlic, salt and pepper in a bowl and mix well. Pour the mixture into the bag, squeeze out the excess air and seal the bag. Place the bag in a shallow pan. Marinate the steak in the refrigerator for 24 hours, turning occasionally.

Remove the steak from the marinade and pat dry with paper towels; reserve the marinade for basting. Place the steak on a preheated grill or a rack in a broiler pan. Broil sirloin steak 4 inches from the heat source for 8 minutes on each side for rare, basting several times with the reserved marinade. (Broil the flank steak for 5 minutes on each side.)

YIELD: 10 SERVINGS

Stuffed Steaks

4 minute steaks
1 egg
5 slices bread
1 (10-ounce) can cream of
   chicken soup

Salt and pepper to taste
2 (10-ounce) cans chicken à la king
¹/₂ cup water

Pound the steaks into a uniform size and thickness and set aside. Beat the egg in a large bowl. Tear the bread into small pieces. Add the torn bread and half the soup and mix until fluffy. Add salt and pepper. Divide the mixture among the steaks and spread to cover. Roll the steaks up to enclose the filling and secure with wooden picks. Place the stuffed steaks in a well-greased 9×9-inch baking dish. Bake at 350 degrees for 45 minutes.

Combine the chicken à la king, remaining soup and water in a bowl and mix well. Pour over the steaks. Reduce the oven temperature to 325 degrees. Bake for 1 hour longer. Place the steaks on a serving plate and remove the wooden picks. Serve with the sauce.

YIELD: 4 SERVINGS

BEEF BURGUNDY

2¹/₂ pounds round steak
¹/₄ cup flour
¹/₄ cup (¹/₂ stick) butter
¹/₂ cup chopped onion
1 tablespoon minced parsley
1 large garlic clove, minced

1 large bay leaf
1 teaspoon salt
Pepper to taste
1 (6-ounce) can mushrooms
1 cup burgundy
³/₄ cup water

Cut the steak into bite-size pieces. Place the flour in a plastic bag. Add the steak and shake until the pieces are well coated. Cook the steak in the butter in a large skillet until brown on all sides. Remove from the heat. Add the onion, parsley, garlic, bay leaf, salt, pepper, mushrooms, burgundy and water and mix well. Simmer, covered, for 1 hour or until the steak is tender, stirring occasionally. Discard the bay leaf before serving.

YIELD: 6 TO 8 SERVINGS

BEEF TENDERLOIN PIE

3 pounds beef tenderloin, cut into
    1-inch cubes
¹/₄ cup (¹/₂ stick) butter
2 tablespoons vegetable oil
3 tablespoons flour
1 (10-ounce) can beef consommé
1 cup dry burgundy
2 medium onions, thinly sliced

1 pound fresh mushrooms, sliced
1 cup chopped celery with leaves
1¹/₂ teaspoons dillweed
1 bay leaf
1 teaspoon Worcestershire sauce
Salt and pepper to taste
1 recipe (1-crust) pie pastry
1 tablespoon melted butter

Brown the beef in a mixture of ¹/₄ cup butter and oil in a large skillet over medium-high heat. Sprinkle with the flour. Add the consommé, burgundy, onions, mushrooms, celery, dillweed, bay leaf, Worcestershire sauce, salt and pepper and mix well. Simmer, covered, for 45 minutes.

Discard the bay leaf. Spoon the mixture into a 2-quart casserole. Cover with the pie pastry, sealing to the edge of the casserole and cutting vents. Brush the pastry with 1 tablespoon melted butter. Bake at 350 degrees for 35 minutes or until the crust is golden brown.

YIELD: 6 SERVINGS

ASPARAGUS AND BEEF CHINESE-STYLE

1 pound fresh asparagus
1 pound flank steak
2 tablespoons vegetable oil
1 teaspoon salt
Pepper to taste

1/3 cup beef bouillon
1 garlic clove, minced
1 tablespoon cornstarch
1/3 cup water

Snap the tough ends from the asparagus and cut the asparagus into thin diagonal slices. Cook the asparagus in boiling water in a saucepan for 5 minutes, drain and set aside. Cut the steak into 1/8-inch slivers. Heat the oil, salt and pepper in a heavy ovenproof skillet over medium-high heat. Add the steak and stir-fry until brown. Remove from the heat. Stir in the bouillon and garlic.

Bake at 350 degrees for 20 minutes. Remove from the oven and place over medium heat. Add the asparagus. Dissolve the cornstarch in the water and stir into the skillet. Cook until thickened, stirring constantly. Serve immediately with hot cooked rice.

YIELD: 4 SERVINGS

SNOWY RIVER CASSEROLE

This casserole takes its name from the high snow-covered hills of Australia's Snowy Mountain region. Australia has larger snowfields than all of Europe—a little-known fact.

2 pounds lean beef, cubed
1/4 cup flour
1 (10-ounce) can tomato soup
1 cup water
2 tablespoons brown sugar

2 tablespoons cider vinegar
2 onions, sliced
2 bay leaves
1/4 cup golden raisins

Coat the beef cubes with flour and place in a large casserole. Combine the soup, water, brown sugar and vinegar in a bowl and mix well. Add the onions, bay leaves and raisins and mix well. Pour the mixture over the beef cubes. Bake, covered, at 350 degrees for 1 1/2 hours. Discard the bay leaves and serve with mashed potatoes and other selected vegetables.

YIELD: 4 TO 6 SERVINGS

Hot Sweet-and-Sour Baked Ribs

2 to 3 pounds boneless beef short ribs
Salt and pepper to taste
1 (8-ounce) can tomato sauce
2 tablespoons molasses
1 teaspoon liquid smoke

1 teaspoon chili powder
2 tablespoons cider vinegar
Cayenne pepper to taste
1 small onion, chopped

Place the ribs in a baking dish just large enough to hold them in a single layer. Sprinkle with salt and pepper. Combine the tomato sauce, molasses, liquid smoke, chili powder, vinegar, cayenne pepper and onion in a saucepan and mix well. Simmer over medium heat for 5 minutes. Pour the mixture over the ribs. Bake, covered, at 275 degrees for 3 hours. Serve over hot cooked noodles.

YIELD: 4 SERVINGS

Sherried Beef

Simple and delicious. Vary by serving over rice, mashed potatoes, toast or noodles.

3 pounds lean beef stew meat
2 (10-ounce) cans cream of
    mushroom soup
3/4 cup sherry

1/2 envelope dry onion soup mix
1 (6- to 8-ounce) can sliced mushrooms
    or 8 ounces fresh mushrooms, sliced
Beef bouillon (optional)

Cut the beef into 1-inch cubes. Mix the soup, sherry and soup mix in a large bowl. Add the beef cubes and mushrooms and stir until coated. Pour the mixture into a 9×13-inch baking pan and cover with foil. Bake at 325 degrees for 3 hours, adding small amounts of bouillon during the cooking time if necessary to make the sauce of the desired consistency.

YIELD: 10 TO 12 SERVINGS

The true cook is the perfect blend, the only perfect blend,
of artist and philosopher.

—*Norman Douglas*

Patchwork Stew

This recipe allows for 4 hours of quality quilting time while it bakes.

2 pounds lean beef stew meat
1 medium onion, chopped
1 cup chopped celery
1 (8-ounce) can sliced water chestnuts, drained
2 cups sliced carrots

2 cups chopped peeled potatoes
2 teaspoons salt
1 tablespoon sugar
2 tablespoons quick-cooking tapioca
1 1/2 cups tomato juice

Cut the beef into bite-size pieces. Spray a roasting pan with nonstick cooking spray. Layer the beef in the bottom of the pan. Add layers of onion, celery, water chestnuts, carrots and potatoes in the order listed. Mix the salt, sugar and tapioca together and sprinkle over the layers. Pour the tomato juice over all. Bake, tightly covered, at 250 degrees for 4 hours. May omit the celery and double the amount of water chestnuts.

YIELD: 6 TO 8 SERVINGS

Veal Stew

2 pounds veal or a mixture of 1/3 beef, 1/3 veal and 1/3 lamb
2 tablespoons flour
3 tablespoons (about) vegetable oil
1 onion, chopped
2 garlic cloves, minced
2 carrots or turnips or parsnips, chopped
2 ribs celery, chopped

1/4 cup flour
1 cup beef broth
1/2 cup red wine
1 bay leaf
1/2 teaspoon each salt and pepper
1 teaspoon dried tarragon
1 teaspoon dried thyme
1/2 teaspoon gravy master
4 potatoes, peeled, cooked, mashed

Cut the veal into 1-inch pieces and toss with the 2 tablespoons flour to coat. Heat the oil in a Dutch oven over medium-high heat. Cook the veal in batches in the hot oil for about 5 minutes or until brown, adding additional vegetable oil as necessary. Set the veal aside. Add the onion, garlic, carrots and celery. Cook over medium heat for 4 minutes, stirring frequently. Sprinkle with the 1/4 cup flour and cook for 1 minute, stirring constantly. Stir in the broth and wine. Bring to a boil, stirring constantly with a wooden spoon to deglaze the pan and scrape up the browned bits. Add the veal, bay leaf, salt, pepper, tarragon, thyme and gravy master and mix well. Reduce the heat and simmer, covered, for 1 hour or until veal and vegetables are very tender. Discard the bay leaf. Serve over the mashed potatoes. Garnish with chopped fresh parsley.

YIELD: 6 TO 8 SERVINGS

French Onion Stew

2½ pounds lean beef stew meat
4 large carrots
3 large ribs celery
12 ounces small white onions
6 ounces fresh mushrooms
1½ cups vegetable juice cocktail
½ cup dry red wine

¼ cup quick-cooking tapioca
1 tablespoon sugar
2 teaspoons salt
1 teaspoon dried basil
¼ teaspoon pepper
2 small bay leaves

Cut the beef into bite-size pieces. Cut the carrots and celery into 2- to 3-inch chunks. Combine the beef and all the vegetables in a 3-quart casserole. Combine the vegetable juice cocktail, wine, tapioca, sugar, salt, basil and pepper in a bowl and mix well. Pour over the beef and vegetables. Place the bay leaves on top. Bake, covered, at 300 degrees for 3 hours, stirring every hour. Discard the bay leaves. If made ahead and refrigerated, bring to room temperature before reheating.

YIELD: 8 SERVINGS

Spiral Meat Loaf

1 pound extra-lean ground beef
1½ cups fresh bread crumbs
2 egg whites
⅓ cup chopped onion
⅓ cup chopped celery
⅓ cup chopped fresh parsley
½ teaspoon salt
¼ teaspoon freshly ground pepper
1 (6-ounce) can mixed vegetable juice

1 tablespoon Worcestershire sauce
1 tablespoon Dijon mustard
1 (10-ounce) package frozen chopped
   spinach, thawed
1 teaspoon salt-free herb seasoning
4 ounces part-skim mozzarella cheese
4 red bell peppers, roasted, peeled, or
   6 jarred roasted red peppers
1 teaspoon salt-free garlic-herb seasoning

Combine the ground beef, bread crumbs, egg whites, onion, celery, parsley, salt, pepper, vegetable juice, Worcestershire sauce and mustard in a bowl and mix well. Pat the mixture into a 10×14-inch rectangle on foil or waxed paper. Drain the spinach and squeeze to remove excess miosture. Spread the spinach over the ground beef rectangle. Sprinkle with the herb seasoning.
   Slice the mozzarella cheese thinly and arrange over the spinach. Seed the roasted peppers and cut into slices. Arrange a layer of peppers over the cheese. Sprinkle with the garlic-herb seasoning. Roll up as for a jelly roll from the short end. Place seam side down in a nonstick baking pan. Tent loosely with foil. Bake at 350 degrees for 35 minutes. Bake, uncovered, for 20 minutes longer or until the juices run clear. Let stand for 5 to 10 minutes before slicing.

YIELD: 8 SERVINGS

Meat Loaf with Brown Sugar and Nutmeg

2/3 cup bread crumbs
2 eggs, beaten
3/4 cup milk
1 1/2 pounds lean ground beef
1/4 cup chopped onion
1 1/2 teaspoons salt

1/2 teaspoon pepper
1/2 teaspoon sage
6 tablespoons brown sugar
1/2 cup ketchup
1/2 teaspoon nutmeg
2 teaspoons dry mustard

Combine the bread crumbs, eggs and milk in a medium bowl and mix well. Add the ground beef, onion, salt, pepper and sage and mix well. Place the ground beef mixture in a loaf pan, smooth the top and poke holes in the mixture.

Combine the brown sugar, ketchup, nutmeg and dry mustard in a small bowl and mix well. Pour the mixture over the loaf. Bake at 350 degrees for 1 hour. Let the loaf stand for 5 to 10 minutes before slicing.

YIELD: 6 SERVINGS

Poor Man's Steak

2 pounds lean ground beef
1 cup cracker crumbs
1 cup 2% milk
1 medium onion, chopped
1 teaspoon salt
1 teaspoon pepper

1 tablespoon flour
1/2 cup vegetable oil
2 (10-ounce) cans cream of mushroom
  soup
1 soup can water

Combine the ground beef, cracker crumbs, milk, onion, salt and pepper in a bowl and mix well. Press into a loaf pan and refrigerate, covered, overnight.

Invert the loaf onto foil or waxed paper and cut into slices of the desired thickness. Coat each slice lightly with flour.

Heat the oil in a large skillet. Brown the slices on both sides in the hot oil. Drain and arrange the slices in a baking dish. Mix the soup and water in a bowl. Spoon the soup mixture over the slices. Bake at 300 degrees for 1 1/2 hours.

YIELD: 10 TO 12 SERVINGS

ITALIAN MEATBALL BOMBERS

1 pound lean ground beef
1 pound bulk Italian sausage
2 garlic cloves, minced
1/2 cup minced onion
4 slices dried Italian bread
2 eggs, lightly beaten
1/2 teaspoon Worcestershire sauce
1 teaspoon Italian seasoning

1/2 teaspoon salt
1/2 teaspoon pepper
1/2 cup grated Romano cheese
1/4 cup chopped fresh parsley
Italian Meat Sauce
10 to 12 buns
Mozzarella cheese, shredded

Combine the ground beef, sausage, garlic and onion in a large bowl. Soak the bread in water, drain and squeeze out the excess moisture. Add the bread, eggs, Worcestershire sauce, Italian seasoning, salt, pepper, Romano cheese and parsley and mix well. Line a baking pan with foil and spray with nonstick cooking spray.

Shape the meat mixture into meatballs of the desired size and arrange in the prepared pan. Bake at 325 degrees for 45 to 60 minutes or until brown. Add the meatballs and the drippings, if desired, to the Italian Meat Sauce. Simmer for 45 minutes.

Place the desired number of meatballs on each bun, add the desired amount of the sauce and top with mozzarella cheese.

YIELD: 10 TO 12 SERVINGS

ITALIAN MEAT SAUCE

8 ounces lean ground beef
8 ounces bulk Italian sausage
3 tablespoons olive oil
1/2 cup chopped onion
1/2 cup chopped green bell pepper
1 garlic clove, minced

1 (12-ounce) can tomato paste
1 (16-ounce) can tomato sauce
1 (15-ounce) can stewed tomatoes
1 beef bouillon cube
2 teaspoons brown sugar

Brown the ground beef and sausage in the olive oil in a large skillet, stirring until crumbly. Add the onion, green pepper and garlic. Stir in the tomato paste, tomato sauce, stewed tomatoes, bouillon cube and brown sugar. Bring to a simmer, stirring until the bouillon cube and brown sugar dissolve.

BERGEDEL GORENG (FRIED MEAT PATTIES)

6 shallots
1 tablespoon (about) butter
4 ounces ground beef
5 large potatoes
1 teaspoon butter
Salt and pepper to taste
1 garlic clove, minced

1 green onion, chopped
1 rib celery, chopped
1 teaspoon butter
1/2 teaspoon nutmeg
Vegetable oil for deep-frying
1 egg white, beaten

Slice the shallots and sauté in the 1 tablespoon butter in a skillet until brown and crisp and set aside. Cook the ground beef in a skillet until brown and crumbly, drain well and set aside. Peel and chop the potatoes. Cook the potatoes in water to cover until tender. Drain the potatoes, add 1 teaspoon butter, salt and pepper and mash until smooth. Add the ground beef, shallots, garlic, green onion, celery, 1 teaspoon butter and nutmeg and mix well.

Heat oil in a deep fryer over medium heat. Shape the ground beef mixture into balls and flatten slightly. Dip the balls into the beaten egg white and deep-fry in the hot oil until golden brown. Drain on paper towels. Serve hot with boiled rice and an assortment of vegetable dishes.

YIELD: 12 TO 15 SERVINGS

BURGER BUNDLES

1 pound ground beef
1 (12-ounce) can evaporated milk
1 cup herb-seasoned stuffing mix
1 (10-ounce) can cream of
   mushroom soup

1 tablespoon ketchup
2 teaspoons Worcestershire sauce

Combine the ground beef and 1/3 cup of the evaporated milk in a bowl and mix well. Divide the mixture into 5 equal portions and flatten each into a 6-inch circle on waxed paper. Combine the stuffing mix with enough of the remaining evaporated milk to moisten. (Reserve any remaining evaporated milk for another purpose and store in the refrigerator.)

Divide the stuffing mixture equally among the ground beef circles. Fold the ground beef over the stuffing to enclose completely and pinch the edges to seal. Place the bundles in a 1 1/2-quart casserole. Bake at 350 degrees for 45 to 50 minutes.

Combine the soup, ketchup and Worcestershire sauce in a saucepan and mix well. Heat the mixture until bubbly. Serve the bundles with mashed potatoes or rice with the soup mixture as gravy. You may substitute cream of celery soup for the mushroom soup.

YIELD: 5 SERVINGS

CABBAGE LASAGNA

2 pounds lean ground beef or turkey
1 medium onion, chopped
1 green bell pepper, chopped
1 medium cabbage
1/2 teaspoon oregano

1 teaspoon salt
1/8 teaspoon pepper
1 (18-ounce) can tomato paste
2 cups (or more) shredded mozzarella
   cheese

Cook the ground beef with the onion and green pepper in a large skillet until brown and crumbly, stirring frequently. Drain the mixture and set aside. Cut the cabbage into bite-size chunks. Bring the cabbage to a boil in water to barely cover in a large saucepan and cook until tender. Drain, reserving 1 cup of the cooking liquid. Place the cooking liquid in a large saucepan and add the oregano, salt, pepper and tomato paste. Simmer over low heat for 5 minutes, stirring occasionally. Add the ground beef mixture and mix well. Ladle half the mixture into a 9×13-inch baking pan. Layer the cabbage evenly in the baking pan and top with the remaining ground beef mixture. Sprinkle the cheese over the top. Bake at 400 degrees for 30 to 45 minutes or until the cheese is brown.

YIELD: 12 SERVINGS

TEXAS-STYLE QUICHE

1 pound ground beef
1/2 cup chopped onion
1 envelope taco seasoning mix
1 cup shredded Cheddar cheese
1 1/4 cups milk

3/4 cup buttermilk baking mix
3 eggs
Shredded lettuce
Sliced tomatoes
Sour cream

Cook the ground beef with the onion in a skillet until the ground beef is brown and crumbly, stirring frequently. Drain and mix in the taco seasoning mix. Spread the mixture evenly in a greased 10-inch pie plate. Sprinkle with the cheese.

Combine the milk, baking mix and eggs in a blender container and process at high speed for 15 seconds or until smooth. Pour over the layers in the pie plate.

Bake at 400 degrees for 25 to 30 minutes or until golden brown and a knife inserted in the center comes out clean. Let the quiche stand for 5 minutes before cutting into wedges. Top with the shredded lettuce and tomato slices and add dollops of sour cream.

YIELD: 6 TO 8 SERVINGS

CALDOONS

An old Russian recipe for filled dumplings.

2¹/₂ cups ground beef
1 tablespoon salt
1 teaspoon pepper
2 eggs, lightly beaten
1 medium onion, finely chopped

4 cups flour
1 teaspoon salt
2 eggs, lightly beaten
1 to 1¹/₂ cups water

Combine the ground beef, 1 tablespoon salt, pepper, 2 eggs and onion in a bowl, mix well and set aside. Mix the flour and 1 teaspoon salt in a large bowl. Add 2 eggs and enough water to make a dough that is soft but not sticky. Roll the dough to ¹/₈-inch thickness on a lightly floured surface and cut with a round biscuit cutter. Place about ¹/₂ teaspoon of the ground beef mixture on each dough circle, fold over to enclose the filling and seal. Bring a large pot of water to a boil. Add about half the dumplings and cook for about 15 minutes. Remove the dumplings with a slotted spoon. Serve in a pasta bowl with lots of salt and pepper and butter for those who like it. Add the remaining dumplings and repeat the process. By the time everyone is ready for a second helping, the second batch should be done.

YIELD: 85 TO 90 DUMPLINGS (6 TO 8 SERVINGS)

PERSIAN EGGPLANT

4 large eggplant
Salt to taste
2 tablespoons margarine
1¹/₂ pounds lean ground beef or lamb
2 onions, chopped

1 bell pepper, chopped
3 ribs celery, chopped
2 garlic cloves, minced
Black pepper and cayenne pepper to taste
Bread crumbs

Peel the eggplant and cut into cubes. Place in a large bowl of cold salted water to cover. Soak for 30 minutes. Drain well. Sauté the eggplant in the margarine in a large skillet until tender and set aside. Sauté the ground beef with the onions, bell pepper, celery and garlic in a large skillet until the ground beef is crumbly and the vegetables are tender. Add the eggplant, salt, black pepper and cayenne pepper to the ground beef mixture and mix well. Add enough bread crumbs to absorb the liquid and mix well. Spoon the mixture into a greased baking dish. Bake at 350 degrees for 30 minutes.

YIELD: 12 SERVINGS

Moussaka

2 medium eggplant
Salt
2 tablespoons olive oil
1 small onion, chopped
1 pound ground beef or lamb

2 garlic cloves, minced
Pepper to taste
$3/4$ to 1 cup tomato juice
2 (15-ounce) cans tomato sauce
2 cups water

Cut the stems from the eggplant and cut into halves lengthwise. Score the pulp of the eggplant halves lengthwise and crosswise at $3/4$-inch intervals to within about $1/2$ inch of the skins. Salt the cut surfaces generously and place scored sides down in a colander. Let drain for 1 hour or longer. Rinse the eggplant halves under cold running water, drain and pat dry with paper towels. Scoop the pulp from the eggplant with a spoon or melon baller to within $1/2$ inch of the skins to form shells. Place the eggplant shells in a lightly greased 9×13-inch baking pan and set aside. Chop the eggplant pulp and set aside.

Heat the olive oil in a large skillet over medium heat. Add the onion and sauté until tender and golden brown. Add the ground beef. Cook until the ground beef is brown, stirring until crumbly. Add the eggplant pulp and garlic. Cook for about 5 minutes, stirring occasionally. Season with salt and pepper. Add the tomato juice and mix well. Simmer, uncovered, until the mixture is moist but not runny. Spoon the mixture into the eggplant shells. Combine the tomato sauce and water in a bowl and mix well. Pour enough of the mixture around the eggplant shells to almost reach the tops of the shells.

Bake at 350 degrees for 45 to 60 minutes or until the eggplant shells are tender, adding tomato sauce or tomato juice as necessary to maintain the level of the sauce. Place the stuffed eggplant on a serving platter. Spoon a small amount of the tomato sauce over the top and serve the remaining sauce in a gravy boat.

YIELD: 4 SERVINGS

I made quilts as fast as I could to keep my family warm, and as pretty
as I could to keep my heart from breaking.

—*From an American pioneer woman's diary*

Macaroni Bake

1 1/2 pounds lean ground beef
1 (15-ounce) can whole kernel corn,
    drained
1 (28-ounce) can diced tomatoes
1 (15-ounce) can whole pitted black
    olives, drained
1 (8-ounce) can tomato sauce
1 tablespoon chili powder
1/2 teaspoon dried thyme leaves, crushed

1/2 teaspoon dried marjoram leaves,
    crushed
1 teaspoon dried sage
1 teaspoon garlic powder
2 teaspoons salt, or to taste
3 1/2 cups water
3 cups uncooked elbow macaroni
4 cups shredded Cheddar cheese

Brown the ground beef in a large skillet, stirring until crumbly; drain and set aside. Combine the corn, undrained tomatoes, drained olives, tomato sauce, chili powder, thyme, marjoram, sage, garlic powder, salt and water in a large saucepan. Bring to a simmer. Add the ground beef and mix well. Stir in the macaroni and pour the mixture into a greased 9×13-inch baking pan. Bake at 350 degrees for 1 hour. Sprinkle the cheese over the top. Bake for 30 minutes longer or until bubbly. Serve with a green or fruit salad and crusty bread.

YIELD: 8 SERVINGS

Four-Cheese Pasta with Roasted Red Peppers

8 ounces ground beef
1 (16-ounce) jar roasted red peppers
1 cup sliced green onions
3 ounces cream cheese
6 ounces penne or other tube-shape pasta

1/2 cup shredded Swiss cheese
1/2 cup shredded Cheddar cheese
1/2 cup shredded Parmesan cheese
Salt and pepper to taste

Brown the ground beef in a large skillet, stirring until crumbly and drain well. Drain the roasted red peppers and add to the ground beef in the skillet, stirring to break up the peppers. Add the green onions and cream cheese and cook over low heat until the cream cheese melts completely. Cook the penne according to the package directions and drain. Place the hot pasta and the shredded cheeses in a large serving bowl, add the ground beef mixture and toss to mix. Cover and let stand for 2 minutes for the cheeses to melt. Add salt and pepper, toss and serve immediately.

YIELD: 4 TO 6 SERVINGS

Mexican Lasagna

1¹/2 pounds lean ground beef
2 tablespoons chili powder
2 teaspoons salt
1 teaspoon pepper
Cumin to taste
1 (15-ounce) can stewed tomatoes
1 egg
2 cups cottage cheese
1 teaspoon garlic powder

1¹/2 cups shredded Monterey Jack cheese
1 (10- to 12-count) package corn tortillas
1¹/2 cups shredded Cheddar cheese
Shredded lettuce
Chopped fresh tomatoes
Sliced black olives
Chopped onion
Jalapeño peppers

Brown the ground beef in a large skillet, stirring until crumbly and drain. Add the chili powder, salt, pepper, cumin and tomatoes and mix well. Cook for about 5 minutes and set aside. Beat the egg in a medium bowl. Add the cottage cheese, garlic powder and Monterey Jack cheese and mix well. Line the bottom and sides of a 9×13-inch baking pan with the tortillas. Spread the ground beef mixture in the prepared pan. Spread the cottage cheese mixture over the ground beef layer. Bake at 400 degrees for 30 to 40 minutes or until the top is brown. Top with the Cheddar cheese, lettuce, tomatoes, olives, onion and jalapeño peppers. Serve with salsa and sour cream.

YIELD: 10 TO 12 SERVINGS

Canadian Meat Pies

1¹/2 pounds ground pork
1¹/2 pounds ground beef
²/3 cup finely chopped onion
2¹/2 teaspoons salt
¹/4 teaspoon pepper

1 teaspoon cinnamon
1 teaspoon cloves
4 potatoes, peeled, cooked, mashed
2 recipes (2-crust) pie pastry

Crumble the ground pork and ground beef into a large skillet. Add the onion, salt, pepper, cinnamon and cloves and enough water to cover. Bring the mixture to a boil and reduce the heat to a simmer. Simmer, uncovered, for 2¹/2 hours, stirring frequently.

Drain the meat mixture, add the mashed potatoes and mix well. Divide the mixture between 2 pastry-lined 9-inch pie plates. Top with the remaining pastry, sealing the edges and cutting vents. Bake at 450 degrees for 10 minutes. Reduce the oven temperature to 350 degrees. Bake for 30 to 35 minutes or until the crusts are golden brown.

YIELD: 6 TO 8 SERVINGS

STUFFED ROAST PORK

1/3 cup chopped scallions
1 garlic clove, minced
2 tablespoons vegetable oil
1 (10-ounce) package frozen chopped
    spinach, thawed
2 eggs, lightly beaten

1 (6-ounce) package herb-seasoned
    stuffing mix
1 (2-pound) boneless rolled pork loin
1 cup apple butter
1/2 cup water

Sauté the scallions and garlic in the oil in a skillet for 2 minutes or until tender but not brown. Add the spinach and cook until heated through, stirring frequently. Remove from the heat and let stand until slightly cooled. Add the eggs, stuffing seasoning and crumbs and mix well. Remove any string from the pork loin so the roast can be opened and laid flat. Spread the stuffing over the pork, roll up to enclose the filling and tie securely with butcher's twine. Place in a roasting pan. Roast at 400 degrees for 10 minutes. Reduce the oven temperature to 350 degrees. Coat the roast with 1/4 cup of the apple butter. Pour the water into the bottom of the roasting pan. Roast, covered, for 45 minutes, adding small amounts of additional water if necessary to prevent the pan from becoming dry. Spread the remaining apple butter over the roast. Roast, uncovered, for 25 minutes longer or until the internal temperature of the roast reaches 145 degrees on a meat thermometer. Let stand for 15 minutes before slicing.

YIELD: 4 TO 6 SERVINGS

BARBECUED PORK SANDWICHES

1 (3-pound) pork loin roast
1 cup water
1 (18-ounce) bottle barbecue sauce
1/4 cup packed brown sugar
2 tablespoons Worcestershire sauce

1 teaspoon salt
1 teaspoon pepper
1 to 2 tablespoons hot sauce, or to taste
20 sandwich buns

Trim the excess fat from the roast, place in a slow cooker and add the water. Cook, covered, on High for 7 hours. Drain the roast, discard the bones and fat and shred the pork with a fork. Pour any liquid from the slow cooker and return the pork to the cooker.

Combine the barbecue sauce, brown sugar, Worcestershire sauce, salt, pepper and hot sauce in a bowl and mix well. Pour the sauce over the pork. Cook, covered, on Low for 1 hour. Serve on the sandwich buns.

YIELD: 20 SANDWICHES

Maple Pork Tenderloin with Stuffing

2 (1¹/₂- to 2-pound) pork tenderloins
Maple Marinade
2 to 3 cups favorite bread stuffing

Salt and pepper to taste
¹/₂ cup maple syrup

Cut the tenderloins lengthwise to, but not through, the opposite side to butterfly. Pour half the Maple Marinade into a 9×13-inch dish. Pierce the tenderloins with a fork in many places over the outside and cut surfaces. Place the butterflied tenderloins open and side by side in the Maple Marinade. Pour the remaining marinade over the tenderloins. Cover with plastic wrap and marinate in the refrigerator for 24 to 48 hours, turning occasionally.

Remove 1 of the tenderloins from the marinade and place cut side up in a 9×13-inch baking dish. Cover evenly with the prepared stuffing. Cover with the remaining tenderloin with the cut side down. Sprinkle with salt and pepper. Bake at 325 degrees for 45 to 60 minutes or until tender, basting with the maple syrup every 15 minutes.

YIELD: 6 SERVINGS

Maple Marinade

³/₄ cup maple syrup
2 tablespoons apple cider vinegar

2 tablespoons minced garlic
1 tablespoon minced fresh rosemary

Blend the maple syrup and vinegar in a bowl. Add the garlic and rosemary and mix well.

Friendship consists in forgetting what one gives, and
remembering what one receives.

—*Alexandre Dumas*

BREADED PORK TENDERLOIN

1 pound pork tenderloin
1 cup flour
Salt and pepper to taste
2 eggs
1 teaspoon water

1 cup seasoned bread crumbs
1/4 cup (1/2 stick) butter
1 large onion, chopped
1/2 cup dry white wine
1 pound fresh mushrooms, sliced

Cut the tenderloin into 1-inch slices and pound to 1/2- to 1/4-inch thickness between waxed paper. Mix the flour, salt and pepper in a shallow dish. Beat the eggs with the water in a shallow dish and place the bread crumbs in a third shallow dish or on waxed paper. Dip the tenderloin slices 1 at a time into the flour mixture to coat on all sides, into the egg mixture and then into the bread crumbs. Melt the butter in an electric skillet at 350 degrees. Cook the breaded tenderloin in the butter until golden brown on both sides. Add the onion and cook just until tender. Add the wine and reduce the heat to a simmer. Simmer, covered, for 15 minutes. Add the mushrooms and simmer for 15 to 20 minutes or until the pork is cooked through. Place the tenderloin on a serving platter and spoon the mushroom sauce over the top. Garnish with tomato slices and parsley sprigs.

YIELD: 4 SERVINGS

PORK TENDERLOIN CASSEROLE

4 to 6 slices bacon, chopped
1 onion, chopped
1 pound pork tenderloin, sliced
Flour
1 or 2 eggs, lightly beaten
Milk
Seasoned bread crumbs

8 ounces fresh mushrooms, sliced
Salt and pepper to taste
1 teaspoon oregano
1 cup beef stock or consommé
1 cup water
2 tablespoons to 1/4 cup white wine

Cook the bacon in a large skillet until brown and crisp. Remove the bacon, reserving the drippings in the skillet; crumble the bacon. Add the onion and sauté until tender. Remove the onion and set aside. Coat the tenderloin slices lightly in a small amount of flour, dip into the egg beaten with a small amount of milk and coat with the seasoned bread crumbs. Cook the tenderloin slices in the bacon drippings until golden brown on both sides and drain well. Discard the bacon drippings. Combine the crisp bacon, sautéed onion, sliced mushrooms, salt, pepper and oregano in a bowl and mix lightly. Alternate layers of the tenderloin and mushroom mixture 1/2 at a time in a 2-quart casserole. Combine the beef stock, water and wine in a bowl and mix well. Pour over the layers. Bake, uncovered, at 325 degrees for 1 hour.

YIELD: 4 SERVINGS

SAUTÉED PORK TENDERLOIN WITH PEACHES

This is a nice change from the usual apples or applesauce served with pork.

2¹/₄ pounds pork tenderloin
¹/₂ cup (about) flour
Salt and pepper to taste
Vegetable oil for frying
¹/₂ cup peach or apricot brandy
1 cup beef broth

1 cup (2 sticks) unsalted butter, chilled
3 ripe peaches or drained canned
   peach slices
¹/₈ teaspoon cinnamon
¹/₈ teaspoon allspice
¹/₈ teaspoon nutmeg

Trim the visible fat from the tenderloin. Slice the tenderloin across the grain into 18 pieces. Pat dry with paper towels and coat with a mixture of flour, salt and pepper. Pour a thin layer of oil into a heavy skillet. Heat the oil over medium heat. Cook the tenderloin in the hot oil until golden brown on both sides and no longer pink. Remove the tenderloin from the skillet and keep warm.

Pour off any fat from the skillet. Tilt the skillet, add the brandy, ignite and allow the flames to subside. Add the broth and deglaze the skillet. Boil until the broth is reduced by ²/₃. Remove the skillet from the heat and whisk in 2 tablespoons of the butter.

Place the skillet over low heat and whisk in the remaining butter 1 tablespoon at a time. Cut the unpeeled peaches into thick slices and add to the skillet. Cook just until the peaches are heated through. Season with the cinnamon, allspice and nutmeg. Place the tenderloin on a serving platter and spoon the peaches and sauce over the top.

YIELD: 6 SERVINGS

You can lay the foundation of a friendship in a matter of moments,
but it is a work of time to build a monument.

—Madelyn Watt

German Pork and Noodles

1 1/2 pounds pork tenderloin
10 slices bacon
1 medium onion, chopped
8 ounces fresh mushrooms, sliced
2 tablespoons whiskey (optional)
1/8 teaspoon cayenne pepper

1/8 teaspoon garlic powder
Salt and black pepper to taste
1 cup heavy cream
1 (12-ounce) package noodles, cooked, drained
1 1/2 cups shredded Parmesan cheese

Cut the tenderloin into bite-size pieces and set aside. Cook the bacon in a large skillet until crisp. Remove the bacon, reserving the drippings in the skillet. Drain the bacon, crumble and set aside. Sauté the onion and mushrooms in the bacon drippings until tender. Remove with a slotted spoon and set aside. Add the tenderloin and sauté until cooked through. Add the whiskey and cook until the whiskey evaporates. Add the seasonings, cream, sautéed vegetables and bacon and mix well. Spread half the noodles in a greased 9×13-inch baking pan. Spoon the tenderloin mixture over the noodles. Add a layer of the remaining noodles and top with the Parmesan cheese. Bake at 450 degrees for 15 minutes.

YIELD: 4 SERVINGS

Pork Chops with Bleu Cheese Stuffing

1/2 cup thinly sliced mushrooms
2 teaspoons minced onion
3 tablespoons butter
1 cup seasoned bread crumbs

1/2 cup crumbled bleu cheese
1/2 cup grated Parmesan cheese
8 thick pork chops with pockets

Cook the mushrooms and onion in the butter in a skillet for about 5 minutes. Remove the skillet from the heat and mix in the bread crumbs, bleu cheese and Parmesan cheese. Spoon the mixture into the pork chop pockets and secure with skewers or wooden picks. Arrange the pork chops in a baking dish and sprinkle with any remaining stuffing. Bake, uncovered, at 325 degrees for 1 hour.

YIELD: 8 SERVINGS

BREADED BAKED PORK CHOPS

6 ($^1/_2$ to $^3/_4$ inch thick) loin pork chops
$^1/_4$ cup melted margarine
$^3/_4$ cup cracker crumbs
$^1/_2$ teaspoon salt

$^1/_4$ teaspoon pepper
$^1/_2$ teaspoon dried thyme
$^1/_2$ teaspoon sage

Trim the fat from the pork chops. Combine the margarine, cracker crumbs, salt, pepper, thyme and sage in a shallow dish and mix well. Coat the pork chops well on all sides with the crumb mixture. Place the pork chops in a single layer on a rack in a shallow baking pan. Bake at 325 degrees for 1$^1/_4$ hours or until golden brown and tender. The coating mixture can be frozen if preparing only 1 or 2 pork chops at a time.

YIELD: 6 SERVINGS

PORK AND CABBAGE

8 thin pork chops
1 head green cabbage
Salt and pepper to taste
1 or 2 (16-ounce) cans whole peeled
    tomatoes

6 tablespoons white vinegar
4 large boiling potatoes

Rinse the pork chops and pat dry. Slice the cabbage thinly or chop coarsely. Alternate layers of the cabbage and 2 pork chops in a large stockpot, salting and peppering each layer. Add the desired amount of tomatoes and the vinegar.

Cook, covered, over low heat for 3 hours, stirring occasionally to prevent sticking if necessary; stir carefully to avoid breaking the chops into pieces. One hour before the cabbage and pork chops are done, scrub the potatoes and cut into halves. Cook the potatoes in boiling salted water to cover in a large saucepan until tender. Serve 1 chop, 1 potato half and a generous helping of cabbage for each serving.

YIELD: 8 SERVINGS

GRILLED ASIAN STICKY RIBS

Once you try this recipe you'll throw away all your other rib recipes.

5 pounds pork spareribs
Salt and pepper to taste

Asian Grilling Sauce

Place the ribs in a large stockpot and add enough water to cover. Bring to a boil over high heat and reduce the heat to low. Simmer, covered, for 45 minutes or just until tender. Drain the ribs and prepare for grilling later in the day by placing the ribs on a large tray, sprinkling with salt and pepper and covering with plastic wrap. Refrigerate until ready to grill.

Heat the grill to medium-high or position the broiler rack 4 to 6 inches from the heat source. Place the ribs on the grill or on a foil-lined broiler pan.

Brush the ribs with half the Asian Grilling Sauce. Grill, covered, or broil for 20 minutes or until tender, turning once and basting occasionally. Ribs should be "sticky-crisp" on the outside and tender on the inside. Serve the remaining sauce at the table for a dipping sauce.

YIELD: 10 SERVINGS

ASIAN GRILLING SAUCE

3/4 cup red wine vinegar
1/2 cup reduced-sodium soy sauce
1/4 cup honey
1/4 cup hoisin sauce
1/4 cup sugar
2 tablespoons toasted sesame oil

3 scallions, chopped
1 tablespoon grated fresh gingerroot, or
    1 teaspoon ground ginger
2 teaspoons chili paste
1 garlic clove, minced

Combine the vinegar, soy sauce, honey, hoisin sauce, sugar, toasted sesame oil, scallions, gingerroot, chili paste and garlic in a saucepan over medium-high heat and mix well. Bring to a boil and reduce the heat to low. Simmer, uncovered, for 15 minutes or until thickened, stirring occasionally.

SWEET-AND-SOUR SPARERIBS

8 to 10 country spareribs
1/2 cup flour
1 teaspoon salt
1/4 teaspoon pepper
1/3 cup vegetable oil
1 (20-ounce) can juice-pack pineapple
  chunks

1 cup orange juice
1/2 cup lemon juice
2 to 3 tablespoons soy sauce
1/2 cup packed brown sugar
2 tablespoons dry mustard

Coat the ribs with a mixture of the flour, salt and pepper. Heat the oil in an electric skillet or a large heavy skillet over high heat. Add the ribs and brown on all sides. Reduce the heat to a simmer. Combine the undrained pineapple, orange juice, lemon juice, soy sauce, brown sugar and dry mustard in a large bowl and mix well. Pour the mixture over the ribs. Simmer, covered, for 1 hour or until tender, basting every 20 minutes with the pineapple mixture. Serve over hot cooked rice.

YIELD: 6 TO 8 SERVINGS

HAM-STUFFED ACORN SQUASH

2 medium acorn squash
1 pound cooked ham, ground
1 egg
1/2 cup soft bread crumbs
1/2 cup chopped celery

1/4 cup chopped green bell pepper
2 tablespoons prepared mustard
1/2 cup packed brown sugar
2 tablespoons butter, softened

Cut the squash into halves; scoop out and discard the seeds. Cut a slice from the bottom of each half to permit the squash to sit firmly in a baking pan.

Combine the ham, egg, bread crumbs, celery, green pepper and mustard in a bowl and mix well. Cream the brown sugar and butter in a small bowl. Divide the brown sugar mixture evenly among the squash halves. Fill the squash with the ham mixture.

Arrange the squash in a shallow baking dish and add water to the dish to a depth of 1 inch. Bake at 350 degrees for 1 to 1 1/2 hours or until the squash is fork-tender.

YIELD: 4 SERVINGS

Red Beans with Rice and Smoked Sausage

The longer this cooks, the better the flavor.

1 pound dried red kidney beans
2 large onions, chopped
2 garlic cloves, minced
1 green bell pepper
1 bottle claret

1/2 cup olive oil
4 ounces ham, chopped
2 pounds smoked sausage
Salt to taste
Steamed rice

Sort and rinse the beans. Place the beans in a large glass or earthenware bowl. Add the onions, garlic and green pepper. Prepare a mixture of half wine and half water. Add enough of the wine mixture to the beans to cover by 1 inch or more. Let the beans soak overnight, adding additional wine mixture if needed. Pour enough of the olive oil into a large heavy kettle to cover the bottom. Add the ham and sausage and cook for several minutes, stirring occasionally. Pour the bean mixture into the kettle. Add additional wine mixture if needed. Bring to a boil and reduce the heat to low. Simmer, covered, for 4 to 5 hours, stirring occasionally and adding additional wine mixture as needed; add salt just before the beans are tender. Serve over steamed rice.

YIELD: 8 TO 10 SERVINGS

Sausage and Green Beans

*Serve this super simple dish over biscuits for a main dish or
as a vegetable side dish in smaller portions.*

1 pound hot or mild sausage
1/4 cup (heaping) flour

2 cups milk
2 quarts cooked green beans, drained

Cook the sausage in a large skillet until brown and crumbly, stirring frequently. Drain the sausage, reserving 1/4 cup of the drippings. Blend the reserved drippings with the flour in a bowl. Stir in the milk. Mix the milk mixture with the sausage in the skillet and cook over medium heat until thickened, stirring constantly. Stir in the green beans and cook until heated through.

YIELD: 8 TO 10 SERVINGS

Jambalaya

1 pound sausage
3/4 cup chopped onion
1/2 cup chopped celery
1/4 cup chopped green bell pepper
1 garlic clove, minced
2 tablespoons margarine
2 cups cubed cooked ham
1 (28-ounce) can chopped tomatoes

1 (10-ounce) can beef broth
1 cup uncooked rice
1 cup water
1 teaspoon sugar
1 teaspoon dried thyme
1/2 teaspoon chili powder
1/4 teaspoon pepper

Cook the sausage in a skillet until brown, stirring until crumbly; drain well. Sauté the onion, celery, green pepper and garlic in the margarine in a Dutch oven until tender. Add the ham, sausage, undrained tomatoes, broth, rice, water, sugar, thyme, chili powder and pepper and mix well. Bring to a boil and reduce the heat. Simmer, covered, for 25 minutes or until the rice is tender.

YIELD: 8 SERVINGS

Sweet-and-Sour Sausage

2 pounds sweet Italian sausage
1 (13-ounce) can pineapple chunks
4 teaspoons cornstarch
1/2 teaspoon salt
1/2 cup maple syrup

1/3 cup water
1/3 cup vinegar
1 large green bell pepper, cut into
   3/4-inch squares
1/2 cup maraschino cherries, drained

Cook the sausage in a skillet until brown on all sides; drain. Cut the sausage into bite-size pieces and set aside. Drain the pineapple, reserving the juice, and set the pineapple aside.

Combine the reserved pineapple juice, cornstarch, salt, maple syrup, water and vinegar in a large saucepan and mix well. Bring to a boil, stirring constantly. Cook until thickened, stirring constantly.

Stir in the sausage, pineapple, green pepper and cherries. Cook for 5 minutes, stirring occasionally. Serve over hot cooked rice.

YIELD: 6 TO 8 SERVINGS

Pizza Quiche

1 recipe (2-crust) pie pastry
4 ounces (about) Italian sausage
1 cup ricotta or cream-style cottage
    cheese
3 eggs
1 cup shredded mozzarella cheese

1/2 cup cubed prosciutto
1/2 cup salami strips
1/2 cup sliced pepperoni
1/4 cup grated Parmesan cheese
1 egg, lightly beaten
2 tablespoons milk

Roll half the pie pastry into a circle on a lightly floured surface. Fit into a deep-dish pie plate and flute the edge. Do not prick the dough. Bake at 450 degrees for 4 to 5 minutes. Remove the pie shell and reduce the oven temperature to 350 degrees. Cook the Italian sausage in a skillet, drain well and slice enough of the sausage to measure 1/2 cup and set aside. Combine the ricotta cheese and 3 eggs in a large bowl and beat until well mixed. Fold in the mozzarella cheese, Italian sausage, prosciutto, salami, pepperoni and Parmesan cheese. Pour the mixture into the partially baked pie shell. Roll the remaining dough into an 8-inch circle and cut into 6 to 8 wedges. Arrange the wedges over the filling. Bake for 20 minutes. Beat 1 egg with the milk and brush over the pastry wedges. Bake for 20 minutes longer. Let stand for 10 minutes before cutting.

YIELD: 6 TO 8 SERVINGS

Sausage Quiche

1 pound sausage
1/2 cup chopped green bell pepper
1/2 cup chopped onion
1 1/2 cups shredded sharp Cheddar cheese
1 tablespoon flour

1 unbaked (9-inch) pie shell
2 eggs
1 cup evaporated milk
1 teaspoon salt
1 teaspoon pepper

Cook the sausage in a skillet until brown and crumbly, stirring frequently. Drain the sausage, reserving 2 tablespoons of the drippings. Sauté the green pepper and onion in the drippings in the skillet until tender.

Toss the cheese with the flour in a bowl. Layer the sausage, green pepper and onion and the cheese in the pie shell. Beat the eggs with the evaporated milk, salt and pepper in a bowl and pour over the layers. Bake at 350 degrees for 35 minutes. Let stand for 5 minutes before cutting into wedges.

YIELD: 6 TO 8 SERVINGS

BACON, ONION AND GARLIC SPAGHETTI

1 pound bacon, chopped
1 large onion, chopped
3 large garlic cloves, chopped
2 (15-ounce) cans diced tomatoes

1 (8-ounce) can tomato sauce
1 (12-ounce) package spaghetti
Freshly shredded Parmesan cheese
    to taste

Cook the bacon in a large skillet until brown and crisp. Remove the bacon with a slotted spoon to drain on paper towels. Pour off the bacon drippings except for a small amount for sautéing. Add the onion and garlic to the skillet and sauté in the reserved bacon drippings until tender. Add the undrained tomatoes and tomato sauce and mix well. Simmer for several minutes. Add the bacon. Simmer, covered, for 25 to 30 minutes. Cook the spaghetti according to the package directions; drain. Combine the spaghetti and sauce in a large bowl and toss to mix. Serve with generous amounts of Parmesan cheese.

YIELD: 4 TO 6 SERVINGS

SPAGHETTI PIE

Assemble the pie ahead and bake at dinnertime if you wish.

1 (6-ounce) package spaghetti
2 eggs, beaten
1/4 cup grated Parmesan cheese
1/3 cup chopped onion
1 tablespoon butter

1 1/4 cups sour cream
1 pound sweet Italian sausage
1 (6-ounce) can tomato paste
1 cup water
1 1/2 cups shredded mozzarella cheese

Break the spaghetti into small pieces. Cook the spaghetti according to the package directions and drain well. Add the eggs and the Parmesan cheese to the warm spaghetti and mix well. Pour the mixture into a 10-inch pie plate sprayed with nonstick cooking spray and press evenly over the bottom and up the side to form a crust. Sauté the onion in the butter in a skillet for 3 to 5 minutes or until tender. Add the sour cream and mix well. Spread the sour cream mixture over the spaghetti crust. Remove the sausage casing. Cook the sausage in a skillet until brown and crumbly, stirring frequently. Drain well. Stir the tomato paste and water into the sausage in the skillet. Simmer for 10 minutes. Spoon the sausage mixture over the sour cream layer. Bake at 350 degrees for 25 minutes. Sprinkle with the mozzarella cheese. Bake for several minutes longer until the cheese melts. Let stand for several minutes before cutting into wedges.

YIELD: 6 TO 8 SERVINGS

PENNE PORTOBELLO

2 cups broccoli florets
2 large portobello mushrooms
1/4 cup (1/2 stick) butter
2 garlic cloves, minced
1/2 cup white wine
4 ounces prosciutto, thinly sliced, chopped

1 (12-ounce) can evaporated milk
2 tablespoons flour
1 (12-ounce) package penne, cooked al dente in salted water, drained
Salt and pepper to taste
2/3 cup freshly grated Parmesan cheese

Steam the broccoli just until tender-crisp. Remove and discard the dark fins on the undersides of the mushrooms and cut the mushrooms lengthwise into 1-inch strips and then into pieces. Sauté the mushrooms in the butter in a large heavy skillet over medium-high heat for 2 minutes. Add the garlic and sauté for 30 seconds. Add the wine and deglaze the skillet. Cook for 4 minutes or until the wine is reduced. Add the prosciutto, broccoli and half the evaporated milk. Cook for 2 minutes. Blend the remaining evaporated milk with the flour, add to the skillet and cook until thickened, stirring constantly. Add the penne and toss. Season with salt and pepper. Pour into a large warmed bowl. Top with Parmesan cheese and serve immediately.

YIELD: 4 SERVINGS

PENNE WITH SAUSAGE AND CREAM SAUCE

1 medium onion, thinly sliced
3 garlic cloves, minced
1 tablespoon butter
1 tablespoon olive oil
1 pound sweet Italian sausage
2/3 cup dry white wine
1 (15-ounce) can diced tomatoes

1 cup heavy cream
1/4 cup chopped Italian parsley
Salt and pepper to taste
1 pound penne, cooked, drained
1 cup freshly grated Parmesan cheese
2 tablespoons chopped Italian parsley

Sauté the onion and garlic in a mixture of the butter and olive oil in a large skillet for 7 minutes or until golden brown. Remove the casing from the sausage and crumble into the skillet. Cook for 7 minutes or until the sausage is brown and crumbly, stirring frequently. Drain the excess drippings. Add the wine to the skillet and cook until the mixture is almost dry, stirring frequently to deglaze the skillet. Add the undrained tomatoes and simmer for about 3 minutes. Stir in the cream and simmer for about 5 minutes or until the sauce is slightly thickened. Stir in the 1/4 cup parsley, salt and pepper. Pour the sauce over the hot cooked penne, add 3/4 cup of the Parmesan cheese and toss to mix. Sprinkle with the remaining 1/4 cup Parmesan cheese and 2 tablespoons parsley.

YIELD: 4 TO 6 SERVINGS

Penne with Sausage and Peppers

1¹/₂ cups uncooked penne
8 ounces mild or spicy Italian sausage
2 green, red or yellow bell peppers, cut
   into ¹/₂-inch strips
1 small onion, coarsely chopped
3 tablespoons olive oil
2 garlic cloves, crushed

2 (15-ounce) cans stewed tomatoes
1 teaspoon dried basil
¹/₂ teaspoon dried oregano
Salt and coarsely ground pepper to taste
Grated Parmesan or Romano cheese
   to taste

Cook the penne according to the package directions until al dente, drain, rinse with cold water, drain well and set aside. Cut the sausage into ¹/₂-inch slices. Cook the sausage in a large skillet over low heat for 10 minutes or until the sausage slices are cooked through and starting to brown. Remove the sausage to drain on paper towels. Discard the drippings and wipe the skillet with paper towels. Sauté the bell peppers and onion in the olive oil in the skillet for 5 minutes or until tender-crisp. Add the garlic and sauté for 1 minute longer. Return the sausage to the skillet. Add the undrained tomatoes, basil, oregano and salt and pepper and mix well. Simmer, covered, for 5 minutes. Add the pasta and mix gently. Heat to serving temperature. Serve with Parmesan cheese.

YIELD: 4 TO 6 SERVINGS

Kielbasa Stir-Fry

1 garlic clove, minced
1 green bell pepper, cut into strips
1 yellow bell pepper, cut into strips
1 large onion, sliced
1 cup sliced fresh mushrooms
1 teaspoon olive oil

1 pound kielbasa or turkey kielbasa
¹/₂ cup sliced black olives
¹/₂ teaspoon sweet basil
¹/₄ teaspoon rosemary
¹/₈ teaspoon Worcestershire sauce

Cook the garlic, bell peppers, onion and mushrooms in the olive oil in a large skillet over medium heat for 15 minutes or until tender, stirring frequently. Cut the kielbasa into bite-size chunks and add to the skillet. Add the olives and cook for 10 minutes, stirring frequently. Add the basil, rosemary and Worcestershire sauce. Cook, covered, over low heat for 10 minutes. Serve over hot cooked brown or white rice.

YIELD: 4 TO 6 SERVINGS

Sausage and Cabbage Stew

Thicken the stew with a small amount of flour if desired, or serve with dumplings.
Adapt the quantities or vegetable selections to suit your taste.

2 slices bacon, chopped
1¹/₂ to 2 pounds kielbasa or other sausage
2 cups coarsely chopped onions
1 cup chopped celery
3 cups water
¹/₄ cup chopped fresh parsley

1 teaspoon peppercorns
5 carrots
5 potatoes
1 small head cabbage
2 teaspoons salt
Ground pepper to taste

Cook the bacon in a skillet until crisp. Remove the bacon and set aside. Cut the sausage into ¹/₄-inch slices. Sauté the sausage, onions and celery in the bacon drippings. Place the sausage mixture, bacon, water and parsley in a stockpot. Place the peppercorns in a teaball or cheesecloth bag; add to stockpot. Cut the carrots, potatoes and cabbage into chunks of the desired size and add to the pot. Add the salt and pepper and mix well. Bring to a boil. Reduce the heat; simmer, covered, until the vegetables are tender. Remove and discard the peppercorns.

YIELD: VARIABLE

Spring Lamb Stew

1 pound lamb stew meat
Salt and pepper to taste
2 tablespoons butter
2 tablespoons flour
12 small boiling onions
5 medium russet potatoes, peeled, quartered

2 large carrots, peeled, cut into 1-inch pieces
10 small bay leaves
2 teaspoons dried thyme
2 cups canned beef broth
¹/₂ cup chopped fresh parsley

Cut the lamb into pieces of the desired size. Sprinkle with salt and pepper. Melt the butter in a Dutch oven over high heat. Add the lamb and sauté for 5 minutes or until brown. Sprinkle with flour. Cook for 2 minutes, stirring constantly. Add the onions, potatoes, carrots, bay leaves and thyme. Cook for 2 minutes, stirring constantly. Add the broth and mix well. Reduce the heat to medium-low and simmer, covered, for 1 hour or until the lamb and vegetables are almost tender. Simmer, uncovered, for 15 minutes or until the lamb and vegetables are very tender and the stew is thickened. Discard the bay leaves. Add the parsley and adjust the seasonings.

YIELD: 4 SERVINGS

ROAST LAMB WITH PEPPERCORN CRUST

3 tablespoons crushed mixed white, black
   and green peppercorns
1 tablespoon minced fresh rosemary
   leaves, or 1¹/₂ teaspoons dried
¹/₂ cup chopped fresh mint leaves
5 garlic cloves, crushed

¹/₂ cup raspberry vinegar
¹/₄ cup oriental soy sauce
¹/₂ cup dry red wine
1 (5-pound) boned leg of lamb, untied
2 tablespoons Dijon mustard

Combine 1 tablespoon of the peppercorn mixture with the rosemary, mint, garlic, vinegar, soy sauce and wine in a shallow bowl. Place the lamb in the marinade, turning to coat. Marinate the lamb, covered, in the refrigerator for 8 hours, turning occasionally. Drain the lamb and reserve the marinade. Roll up the lamb and secure with butcher's twine. Spread the mustard over the lamb and press the remaining peppercorn mixture into the mustard. Place in a shallow roasting pan just big enough to hold the lamb. Pour the reserved marinade around but not over the lamb. Roast at 350 degrees for 18 minutes per pound for medium-rare, basting occasionally. Let stand for 20 minutes before slicing. Serve with the pan juices.

YIELD: 6 TO 8 SERVINGS

LAMB-STUFFED EGGPLANT

3 eggplant
¹/₂ cup (about) butter
1 pound ground lamb
1 onion, chopped
¹/₂ cup (about) butter

¹/₂ cup pine nuts
Allspice, nutmeg and cinnamon
   to taste
Salt and pepper to taste
1 (12-ounce) can tomato purée

Peel the eggplant and cut each into quarters lengthwise. Sauté the eggplant in about ¹/₂ cup butter in a large skillet until tender. Place the eggplant pieces side by side in a shallow baking pan and cut a pocket in the center of each. Set the eggplant aside.

Cook the lamb and onion in about ¹/₂ cup butter in the skillet until the lamb is brown and crumbly, stirring frequently. Remove the lamb and onion with a slotted spoon and place in a bowl. Brown the pine nuts in the drippings, remove with a slotted spoon and add to the lamb mixture. Season the lamb mixture with the allspice, nutmeg, cinnamon, salt and pepper and mix well.

Fill the eggplant pockets with the lamb mixture. Pour the tomato purée over the stuffed eggplant. Bake at 350 degrees for 20 minutes.

YIELD: 3 TO 6 SERVINGS

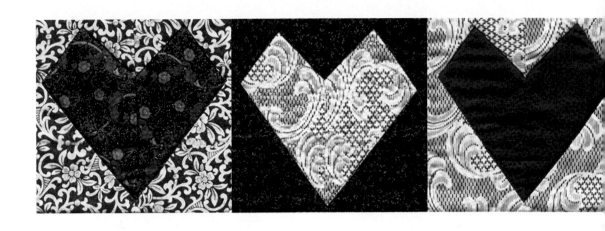

POULTRY,
SEAFOOD AND
MEATLESS ENTRÉES

Timeless Hearts Quilt

31" × 35"

In the last half of the nineteenth century, blue-and-white quilts enjoyed great popularity. A quiltmaker's "best" quilt—the one that showcased her fanciest quilting and was saved for special occasions—was often done in blue and white. But the appeal of this wonderful color combination knows the limits of neither borders nor time. From Chinese porcelain to French toiles to the most contemporary of decorating schemes, this tried-and-true color combination is always fresh and up-to-date. It's no surprise that quilters have fallen in love with the graphic look and limitless design possibilities of this elegant two-color palette.

It's simple…it's formal. It's old-fashioned…it's modern. But above all, a blue-and-white quilt is classic. Its timeless appeal creates a bond between quiltmakers of the past and present.

Skillet Barbecued Chicken

Especially good with mashed potatoes or brown rice.

1 (3-pound) chicken
1 medium onion, chopped
1 tablespoon vegetable oil
1/2 cup ketchup
1/2 cup water
2 tablespoons brown sugar

2 tablespoons vinegar
1 1/2 tablespoons Worcestershire sauce
1/2 teaspoon salt
1/2 teaspoon celery salt
1/2 teaspoon chili powder

Cut the chicken into pieces and set aside. Sauté the onion in the oil in a large skillet until tender. Add the ketchup, water, brown sugar, vinegar, Worcestershire sauce, salt, celery salt and chili powder and mix well. Bring the mixture to a boil.

Arrange the chicken pieces in the skillet and reduce the heat to a simmer. Simmer, covered, for 30 minutes. Simmer, uncovered, for 15 minutes or until the chicken is tender, turning occasionally.

YIELD: 4 TO 6 SERVINGS

Sweet-and-Sour Chicken

The best sweet-and-sour chicken this side of your favorite oriental restaurant.

1 cup sugar
3 tablespoons ketchup
1 tablespoon soy sauce
2 beef or chicken bouillon cubes
1 cup flour

1/2 cup cornstarch
2 eggs
1 chicken, cut up, or boneless skinless
    chicken breasts
Vegetable oil for frying

Combine the sugar, ketchup, soy sauce and bouillon cubes in a saucepan over medium heat. Heat until the sugar and bouillon cubes dissolve and the mixture is smooth, stirring frequently.

Mix the flour and cornstarch in a shallow dish. Beat the eggs in a shallow dish. Dip the chicken into the beaten eggs and then into the flour mixture to coat. Brown the chicken on all sides in hot oil in a skillet and arrange the chicken in a baking dish. Pour the sauce over the chicken. Bake at 375 degrees for 45 minutes, basting occasionally. Serve with hot cooked rice.

YIELD: 4 TO 6 SERVINGS

CHEESY BROCCOLI CHICKEN

1¹/₂ pounds fresh broccoli spears, or
   1 (20-ounce) package frozen
   broccoli spears, thawed
4 boneless skinless chicken breasts
1 (10-ounce) can cream of
   mushroom soup

1 cup mayonnaise
1 (8-ounce) can sliced water chestnuts,
   drained
1 pound Velveeta cheese, cubed
1 (3-ounce) can French-fried onions

Parboil the fresh broccoli for 5 minutes, drain well and arrange in a single layer in a greased 9×13-inch baking dish.

Cut the chicken into bite-size pieces and layer over the broccoli. Combine the soup and mayonnaise in a bowl and mix well. Spoon the mixture over the chicken. Add layers of the water chestnuts and cheese cubes.

Bake at 350 degrees for 40 minutes. Top with a layer of the onions. Bake for 15 minutes longer. Serve over hot cooked rice.

YIELD: 8 SERVINGS

CHICKEN AND CORNED BEEF BAKE

2 (2-ounce) packages dried corned beef
10 boneless skinless chicken breasts
1 pound sliced bacon

2 cups sour cream
2 (10-ounce) cans cream of
   mushroom soup

Shred the corned beef and spread over the bottom of a greased 9×13-inch baking dish. Wrap each of the chicken breasts in bacon slices and secure with wooden picks. Arrange the chicken on the bed of corned beef. Combine the sour cream and soup in a bowl and mix well. Spoon over the chicken. Bake at 275 degrees for 3 hours.

YIELD: 10 SERVINGS

Yes'm, old friends is always best, 'less you can catch a new one
that's fit to make an old one out of.

—*Sarah Orne Jewett*

White Chili

Pass the hot pepper sauce for guests who want gusto.

1 onion, chopped
1 garlic clove, minced
1 teaspoon ground cumin
1 tablespoon vegetable oil
4 boneless skinless chicken breasts
1 (16-ounce) can cannellini beans
1 (16-ounce) can garbanzo beans

1 (16-ounce) can whole kernel white corn
2 chicken bouillon cubes
2 (4-ounce) cans chopped green chiles
1 1/2 cups water
Shredded Monterey Jack cheese
Chopped fresh chives or parsley

Sauté the onion, garlic and cumin in the oil in a Dutch oven for 3 minutes. Cut the chicken into the desired size cubes. Add the chicken to the sautéed vegetables and cook for 10 minutes, stirring occasionally. Add the beans, corn, bouillon cubes, green chiles and water and mix well. Simmer, covered, on the stovetop or bake, covered, in a 350-degree oven for 1 hour. Ladle into soup bowls and serve with a sprinkle of cheese and chives.

YIELD: 4 OR 5 SERVINGS

Chicken Enchiladas

1/2 cup mayonnaise-type salad dressing
1/4 cup lime juice
1 envelope taco seasoning mix
8 boneless skinless chicken breasts
1 cup mayonnaise-type salad dressing
2 teaspoons ground cumin

1/2 teaspoon ground red pepper
12 (6-inch) flour tortillas
2 (12-ounce) jars salsa
2 cups shredded Cheddar cheese
2 tablespoons chopped cilantro

Combine 1/2 cup salad dressing, lime juice and taco seasoning mix in a bowl and mix well. Arrange the chicken on a broiler pan and brush the chicken with half the salad dressing mixture. Broil 5 to 7 inches from the heat source for 8 to 10 minutes. Turn the chicken over and brush with the remaining mixture. Broil for 8 to 10 minutes or until tender. Cut the chicken into cubes.

Combine 1 cup salad dressing, cumin and red pepper in a large bowl and mix well. Add the chicken cubes and mix well. Spoon about 1/3 cup of the chicken mixture onto each tortilla, roll up to enclose the filling and place seam side down in two 8×12-inch baking dishes. Spoon the salsa over the filled tortillas. Sprinkle with the cheese. Bake at 350 degrees for 30 minutes. Sprinkle with the cilantro.

YIELD: 8 SERVINGS

Enchiladas Fantastic

1 pound ground turkey
1 cup salsa
1 (10-ounce) package frozen chopped
    spinach, thawed
8 ounces cream cheese

10 (7-inch) flour tortillas
1 (15-ounce) can diced tomatoes
1 cup salsa
1 cup shredded Cheddar cheese

Cook the ground turkey in a large skillet, stirring until crumbly, and drain well. Add 1 cup salsa. Drain the spinach and squeeze dry. Add to the skillet and mix well. Cook for 5 minutes. Chop the cream cheese, add to the skillet and cook until the cream cheese melts, stirring constantly. Spoon about 1/3 cup of the mixture onto each tortilla, roll up to enclose the filling and place seam side down in a 9×13-inch baking dish. Combine the tomatoes and 1 cup salsa in a bowl and mix well. Spoon over the filled tortillas. Bake at 350 degrees for 20 minutes. Sprinkle the cheese over the top. Bake for 2 minutes longer or until the cheese melts. Top with a garnish of shredded lettuce, sour cream, chopped onions or sliced olives.

YIELD: 5 SERVINGS

Chicken from Heaven

By the time you serve this dish there is absolutely no alcohol left—just delicious flavor.

1 chicken
2 chicken breasts
Salt and pepper to taste
2 to 3 garlic cloves, minced
1/2 cup (1 stick) butter
3 cups white vermouth or white wine
4 large tomatoes, quartered

1 1/2 cups heavy cream
2 tablespoons minced fresh rosemary
1 tablespoon minced fresh thyme
1 teaspoon minced fresh marjoram
    (optional)
1 tablespoon (about) cornstarch

Cut the whole chicken into 6 pieces. Sprinkle all the chicken with salt and pepper and set aside. Sauté the garlic in the butter in a large heavy skillet over high heat for several seconds. Add the chicken pieces and brown on all sides. Add the vermouth and tomatoes. Bring to a boil and reduce the heat to medium-low. Simmer, covered, for 70 minutes or until the chicken is tender. Remove the chicken. Stir in the cream, rosemary, thyme and marjoram and mix well. Dissolve enough cornstarch to thicken the sauce as desired in a small amount of cold water. Stir the cornstarch mixture into the sauce and cook until thickened, stirring constantly. Return the chicken to the skillet. Heat to serving temperature. Serve with hot cooked rice and a fresh salad.

YIELD: 4 TO 8 SERVINGS

MARINATED CHICKEN BREASTS

$^1/_2$ cup lime juice
1 cup olive oil
1 cup honey
3 tablespoons chopped fresh cilantro
2 tablespoons dried oregano
1 tablespoon salt

$1^1/_2$ teaspoons ground cumin
3 garlic cloves, mashed
3 fresh jalapeño peppers, seeded, finely chopped (optional)
8 boneless skinless chicken breasts

Combine the lime juice, olive oil, honey, cilantro, oregano, salt, cumin, garlic and jalapeño peppers in a saucepan and mix well. Bring to a simmer and simmer for 10 to 15 minutes, stirring occasionally. Let stand until cool. Place the chicken in a shallow dish. Pour the cooled mixture over the chicken, covering completely. Marinate, covered, in the refrigerator overnight.

Drain the chicken, reserving the marinade. Grill the chicken over medium-hot coals until tender and the juices run clear. Heat the reserved marinade to the boiling point in a saucepan. Simmer for several minutes and serve on the side.

YIELD: 8 SERVINGS

GARLIC CHICKEN PASTA

5 slices bacon
1 medium onion, thinly sliced
4 garlic cloves, minced
4 boneless skinless chicken breasts
1 tablespoon flour
$1^1/_2$ cups chicken broth

$^1/_4$ cup sour cream
$^1/_4$ cup shredded Italian cheese mix
Salt and pepper to taste
8 ounces angel hair pasta, cooked
Chopped fresh parsley to taste
$^1/_4$ cup grated Parmesan cheese

Fry the bacon in a large skillet until crisp. Remove the bacon to drain on paper towels. Sauté the onion in the bacon drippings in the skillet until tender. Add the garlic. Cut the chicken into the desired size chunks and add to the skillet. Cook, covered, over medium-low heat for 20 minutes or until the chicken is tender.

Sprinkle the flour over the top and cook for 1 minute, stirring constantly. Stir in the broth. Cook until the sauce thickens, stirring constantly. Whisk the sour cream into the sauce. Add the Italian cheese mix, salt and pepper and stir until the cheese melts. Toss the chicken mixture with the pasta in a large bowl. Top the individual servings with crumbled bacon, parsley and Parmesan cheese.

YIELD: 4 SERVINGS

Sherried Mushroom Chicken with Consommé Rice

*Try substituting apricot nectar for the sherry for a different
but equally easy chicken dish.*

8 boneless skinless chicken breasts
1 (6-ounce) can sliced mushrooms,
   drained
¼ cup dry sherry

1 cup sour cream
1 (10-ounce) can cream of
   chicken soup

Arrange the chicken in a 9×13-inch baking dish and add the mushrooms. Combine the sherry,
sour cream and soup in a bowl and mix well. Spoon over the chicken and mushrooms. Bake,
uncovered, at 350 degrees for about 1 hour or until the chicken is tender and the top is brown.
Serve with Consommé Rice.

YIELD: 4 TO 8 SERVINGS

Consommé Rice

1 cup uncooked rice
1 cup consommé
1 cup water

½ envelope dry onion soup mix
2 tablespoons margarine
1 (4-ounce) can sliced mushrooms

Combine the rice, consommé, water, soup mix, margarine and mushrooms in a baking dish.
Bake, covered, at 350 degrees for 1 hour.

When you educate a man you educate an individual; when
you educate a woman you educate a whole family.

—*R. M. MacIver*

Chicken Stir-Fry

2 boneless skinless chicken breasts
1 cup chicken broth
1/4 cup soy sauce
2 tablespoons dry sherry
2 tablespoons cornstarch
1/4 teaspoon garlic powder

1/4 teaspoon ground ginger
1 tablespoon vegetable oil
1/2 cup (1-inch pieces) green onions
1/2 cup sliced celery
1 cup sliced fresh mushrooms
1/2 tomato, seeded, chopped

Cut the chicken into bite-size pieces. Combine the broth, soy sauce, sherry, cornstarch, garlic powder and ginger in a small bowl, mix well and set aside. Heat the oil in a heavy skillet or wok over medium-high to high heat. Add the chicken and stir-fry for 3 to 5 minutes. Add the green onions, celery and mushrooms and stir-fry for 5 minutes. Add the broth mixture and cook until thickened, stirring constantly. Add the tomatoes and cook just until heated through, stirring constantly. Serve immediately over hot cooked rice.

YIELD: 2 SERVINGS

Teriyaki Chicken with Cashews

2 pounds boneless skinless chicken breasts
1/4 cup reduced-sodium soy sauce
1/4 cup teriyaki sauce
2 tablespoons hot sauce
2 tablespoons Worcestershire sauce
1 tablespoon onion powder
1 teaspoon garlic powder
1/2 teaspoon nutmeg

1/4 teaspoon ground ginger
1 cup water
2 to 3 tablespoons cornstarch
1/4 cup water
2 tablespoons olive oil
2 cups steamed broccoli florets
1/3 cup maple syrup
1/2 cup cashews

Cut the chicken breasts into thin slices and set aside. Combine the soy sauce, teriyaki sauce, hot sauce, Worcestershire sauce, onion powder, garlic powder, nutmeg and ginger in a small bowl and mix well. Stir in 1 cup water and set aside. Dissolve the cornstarch in 1/4 cup water and set aside. Heat the olive oil in a large heavy skillet or wok over high heat. Add the chicken and stir-fry for 5 to 8 minutes or until the chicken is cooked through. Add the broccoli and stir-fry for several seconds. Add the soy sauce mixture and the syrup and cook until the mixture comes to a boil. Stir in the cornstarch mixture and cook until thickened, stirring constantly. Add the cashews and cook just until the cashews are heated through. Serve over hot cooked rice or angel hair pasta.

YIELD: 8 SERVINGS

Chicken Loaf Supreme

The loaf unmolds beautifully with a crispy brown crust that always impresses guests.

1 (4-pound) chicken
2 cups soft bread crumbs
3/4 cup uncooked rice
1 tablespoon salt

3 eggs, well beaten
1/4 cup (1/2 stick) butter, cut into pieces
1/2 cup sliced mushrooms or pimentos or
    a mixture of both

Boil the chicken as desired until tender. Drain and cool the chicken and reserve the stock. Bone and chop the chicken. Strain enough of the stock to measure 3 cups and set aside. (Add enough milk to measure 3 cups if necessary. Reserve any remaining stock for another purpose.) Combine the chopped chicken, bread crumbs, rice, salt, eggs, chicken stock, butter and mushrooms in a large bowl and mix well. Spoon the mixture into a greased bundt pan or 2-quart casserole.

Bake at 350 degrees for 1 1/2 hours. Cool in the pan for 3 to 4 minutes. Loosen from the side of the pan and invert onto a serving platter. Garnish with parsley, candied apple slices or fresh orange sections. May serve with a mushroom sauce or tomato sauce made by heating canned soup with 3/4 cup milk.

YIELD: 8 TO 10 SERVINGS

Chicken Avocado Boats

Bite-size fresh vegetables with a tangy dip serve as a good texture and flavor accompaniment for this surprisingly delicious and filling dish.

3 large ripe avocados
6 tablespoons lemon juice
3/4 cup mayonnaise
1 1/2 tablespoons grated onion
1/4 teaspoon celery salt

1/4 teaspoon garlic powder
Salt and pepper to taste
2 cups chopped cooked chicken
1/2 cup shredded Cheddar cheese

Cut the avocados into halves, remove the pits but do not peel. Sprinkle each half with about 1 tablespoon of the lemon juice, covering the cut surfaces completely to prevent browning. Combine the mayonnaise, onion, celery salt, garlic powder, salt and pepper in a medium bowl and mix well. Stir in the chicken. Drain any lemon juice from the avocados and place in a 9×13-inch baking dish. Spoon the chicken mixture into the avocados and sprinkle with the cheese. Pour water to a depth of 1/2 inch into the baking dish. Bake at 350 degrees for 15 minutes or until the cheese melts. Serve immediately. Garnish with snipped chives.

YIELD: 6 SERVINGS

CHICKEN AND WILD RICE

1 (6-ounce) package long grain and wild
  rice mix
2 (10-ounce) packages frozen chopped
  broccoli, thawed
2 cups chopped cooked chicken
1 (8-ounce) can sliced water chestnuts,
  drained

1 (10-ounce) can cream of celery soup
1/2 cup mayonnaise
1/2 cup yogurt or sour cream
2 tablespoons prepared mustard
1 teaspoon curry powder
1/4 cup grated Parmesan cheese
1 cup shredded Cheddar cheese

Prepare the rice mix according to the package directions. Drain the broccoli. Layer the
prepared rice mix, chicken, water chestnuts and broccoli in a lightly greased 9×13-inch baking
dish. Combine the soup, mayonnaise, yogurt, mustard and curry powder in a bowl and mix
well. Spread the mixture over the layers. Sprinkle with a mixture of the Parmesan and Cheddar
cheeses. Bake at 350 degrees for 25 to 30 minutes or until bubbly and golden brown.

YIELD: 8 SERVINGS

CHICKEN AND SHRIMP STROGANOFF

4 large boneless skinless chicken breasts
8 ounces peeled large shrimp
2 tablespoons margarine or butter
1/4 teaspoon salt
1 tablespoon margarine or butter
8 ounces mushrooms, sliced
2 tablespoons dry sherry

2 tablespoons flour
1/8 teaspoon pepper
2 teaspoons instant chicken bouillon
1 cup each water and sour cream
1 tablespoon chopped fresh parsley
1 (16-ounce) package wide noodles
Butter

Cut the chicken into 1-inch cubes and set aside. Rinse the shrimp and drain well. Sauté the
shrimp in 2 tablespoons margarine in a large skillet over medium heat for about 5 minutes or
just until the shrimp turn pink. Remove the shrimp and set aside. Add the chicken to the
skillet and sauté until the chicken is lightly browned and the juices run clear. Sprinkle with the
salt and add the chicken to the shrimp. Add 1 tablespoon margarine to the skillet drippings
and add the mushrooms and sherry. Sauté for several minutes. Combine the flour, pepper,
instant bouillon and water in a small bowl and mix until well blended. Stir into the mushroom
mixture and cook until thickened, stirring constantly. Reduce the heat and stir in the sour
cream. Return the shrimp and chicken to the skillet. Heat to serving temperature but do not
boil. Cook the noodles according to the package directions, drain and add the desired amount
of butter, tossing to coat. Serve the stroganoff over the noodles.

YIELD: 6 SERVINGS

SEASIDE DINNER

2 medium potatoes
1 rib celery
1/2 green bell pepper
1/2 onion
1 teaspoon salt
1 teaspoon dillweed
1 teaspoon dried basil leaves

1/4 teaspoon pepper
1 pound flounder fillets or other
   white fish
1 to 2 tablespoons butter
1 or 2 tomatoes
Lemon wedges

Peel the potatoes and cut into 1/4-inch slices. Slice enough of the celery into 1/4-inch diagonal slices to yield 1/2 cup. Cut enough of the green pepper into 1/2×2-inch strips to yield 1/2 cup. Slice enough of the onion into 1/4-inch slices to yield 1/2 cup. Layer the potatoes, celery, green pepper and onion in an ungreased 9-inch square baking dish. Sprinkle with half of each of the seasonings. Arrange the fillets skin side down in the baking dish to cover all the vegetables. Sprinkle with the remaining seasonings and dot with the butter. Bake, covered with foil, at 425 degrees for 40 to 50 minutes or until the fish flakes easily and the vegetables are tender. Remove the foil. Slice the tomatoes 1/4 inch thick and arrange over the fish. Bake, uncovered, for 3 to 5 minutes or until the tomatoes are heated through and firm. Serve with lemon wedges.

YIELD: 4 SERVINGS

BAKED STUFFED TROUT

1/2 cup water
2 tablespoons butter
1 cup savory herb-seasoned
   stuffing mix
1 (6-ounce) can crab meat, drained

1 egg
1/2 cup shredded Monterey Jack cheese
Bread crumbs (optional)
2 (1 1/2-pound) trout, cleaned
2 tablespoons butter

Bring the water and 2 tablespoons butter to a boil in a saucepan. Add the stuffing mix and mix until moistened. Place the stuffing in a medium bowl. Add the crab meat, egg and cheese and mix well. Add a small amount of bread crumbs to the stuffing mixture to make the desired consistency. Spoon the stuffing mixture into the trout cavities.

Place the trout in a greased 9×13-inch baking dish. Dot with 2 tablespoons butter. Bake, covered with foil, at 375 degrees for 30 minutes. Bake, uncovered, for 30 minutes longer or until the fish flakes easily.

YIELD: 4 SERVINGS

SALMON SCALLOP

1 (15-ounce) can salmon
1 tablespoon fresh lemon juice
Milk
1¹/₃ cups butter cracker crumbs
¹/₃ cup margarine or butter
¹/₄ teaspoon pepper
¹/₂ teaspoon dry mustard
¹/₄ teaspoon dried thyme

1 tablespoon dried onion flakes (optional)
2 tablespoons margarine or butter
1 tablespoon flour
¹/₂ cup (or more) milk
¹/₂ cup shredded Cheddar, American or
   Swiss cheese
Salt and pepper to taste

Drain the salmon, reserving the liquid. Combine the reserved liquid, lemon juice and enough milk to measure 1 cup and set aside. Combine the cracker crumbs, ¹/₃ cup margarine, ¹/₄ teaspoon pepper, dry mustard, thyme and onion flakes in a bowl and mix until crumbly. Spread half the crumb mixture in a greased 8-inch square baking dish. Flake the salmon and layer over the crumb layer. Pour the milk mixture over the layers and top with the remaining crumb mixture. Bake at 375 degrees for 25 to 30 minutes or until brown. Melt 2 tablespoons margarine in a small saucepan. Blend in the flour. Stir in enough of the ¹/₂ cup milk to make the sauce of the desired consistency. Cook until smooth and thickened, stirring constantly. Add the cheese, salt and pepper to taste and heat until the cheese is melted, stirring constantly. Serve immediately with the salmon.

YIELD: 4 SERVINGS

SHRIMP WITH CAJUN GRAVY

Also very good served over toast, potatoes or biscuits.

1 rib celery, chopped
¹/₂ onion, or 2 green onions, chopped
¹/₂ green bell pepper, chopped
1 tablespoon minced parsley
¹/₂ cup (1 stick) margarine
2 (10-ounce) cans cream of
   mushroom soup

2 cups half-and-half
4 ounces baby Swiss cheese, shredded
4 ounces Velveeta cheese, chopped
¹/₂ teaspoon garlic powder
Salt, pepper and red pepper to taste
1 to 2 pounds shrimp or crawfish tails,
   cooked, peeled

Sauté the celery, onion, green pepper and parsley in margarine in a large saucepan until tender. Add the soup, half-and-half, Swiss and Velveeta cheese and seasonings and mix well. Cook until the cheese melts, stirring constantly. Stir in the shrimp. Cook for 10 to 15 minutes, stirring frequently. Serve over hot cooked penne.

YIELD: 4 SERVINGS

Skillet Bouillabaisse

2 medium onions, chopped
2 garlic cloves, mashed
1/4 cup vegetable oil
2 (16-ounce) cans stewed tomatoes with
    Italian seasonings
2 cups water
1 1/2 teaspoons salt

1/2 teaspoon pepper
1/2 teaspoon dried thyme
1/2 teaspoon paprika
2 tablespoons chopped fresh parsley
3 pounds frozen scallops or peeled shrimp
    or mixture of both

Sauté the onions and garlic in the oil in a large skillet until tender but do not brown. Add the tomatoes, water, salt, pepper, thyme, paprika and parsley. Simmer for 10 minutes. Add the scallops. Cook for about 5 minutes or until the scallops are tender. Serve with hot cooked pasta of choice and French bread.

YIELD: 6 SERVINGS

Seafood Risotto

1/2 cup finely chopped onion
1 garlic clove, minced
1 tablespoon olive oil
1 cup uncooked long grain rice
2 cups chicken broth
1/2 cup chopped zucchini

8 ounces uncooked medium shrimp
8 ounces scallops
1 cup frozen peas, thawed
1/4 cup minced fresh parsley
1/4 cup grated Parmesan cheese

Sauté the onion and garlic in the olive oil in a large heavy skillet over medium heat until tender. Add the rice and sauté for about 3 minutes or until opaque. Add 1 cup of the broth. Bring to a boil and reduce the heat. Simmer, covered, for 10 minutes or until the liquid is absorbed. Stir in the remaining 1 cup broth and the zucchini. Simmer, covered, for 5 minutes.

Peel the shrimp, devein and cut lengthwise into halves. Cut the scallops into halves. Add the shrimp, scallops and peas to the rice mixture. Simmer, covered, for 10 minutes, stirring once. Stir in the parsley and cook for 5 minutes longer or until the liquid is absorbed, the rice is tender and the shrimp and scallops are opaque. Stir in the Parmesan cheese and serve immediately.

YIELD: 4 SERVINGS

SHRIMP SCAMPI

3 tablespoons butter
3 tablespoons olive oil
2 teaspoons garlic powder

2 teaspoons seasoned salt
8 ounces uncooked peeled shrimp

Melt the butter in a skillet. Add the olive oil and seasonings. Add the shrimp and cook over medium heat for about 5 minutes or until the shrimp turn pink. Pour the pan drippings over hot cooked linguini and arrange the shrimp on top.

YIELD: 2 SERVINGS

PENNE WITH SHRIMP AND ASPARAGUS

The lemon-based sauce is a flavorful surprise. It is a great way to herald spring when fresh asparagus is abundant.

1 pound uncooked medium shrimp
1/2 cup mayonnaise
1/2 cup chicken broth
1 teaspoon grated lemon peel
2 tablespoons fresh lemon juice
2 tablespoons vegetable oil

1 tablespoon grated peeled gingerroot
2 garlic cloves, minced
1 pound fresh asparagus, sliced diagonally
1 (16-ounce) package penne, cooked, drained
1/2 teaspoon lemon pepper

Peel and devein the shrimp and set aside. Combine the mayonnaise, broth, lemon peel and juice in a small bowl, whisk until well blended and set aside. Heat the oil in a large heavy skillet or wok. Add the gingerroot and garlic and sauté for 1 minute. Add the shrimp and asparagus. Sauté until the shrimp turn pink. Add the mayonnaise mixture and the penne and toss until well mixed. Sprinkle with the lemon pepper and serve immediately.

YIELD: 6 TO 8 SERVINGS

When life gives you scraps, make a quilt!

Lemon and Garlic Pasta with Shrimp

2 teaspoons minced garlic
1/4 cup olive oil
2 tablespoons butter
1 teaspoon grated lemon peel
1 to 2 tablespoons fresh lemon juice
6 mushrooms, sliced

24 grape tomatoes
24 uncooked peeled shrimp
Salt and pepper to taste
1/4 cup chopped fresh parsley or basil
8 ounces spaghetti, cooked, drained

Sauté the garlic in a mixture of the olive oil and butter in a large skillet for 1 minute. Add the lemon peel and juice, mushrooms and tomatoes. Sauté for 3 minutes. Add the shrimp and cook just until pink. Add salt and pepper, parsley and pasta and toss until well mixed. Serve immediately with grated Parmesan cheese.

YIELD: 4 SERVINGS

Spinach Lasagna

This healthy dish will be a family favorite. It can be prepared the day
before baking and refrigerated until baking time.

2 cups nonfat cottage cheese
2 cups shredded part-skim mozzarella
    cheese
1/2 cup grated Parmesan cheese
1 (10-ounce) package frozen chopped
    spinach, cooked

2 eggs, well beaten
1 (26-ounce) jar pasta sauce
9 lasagna noodles, cooked
1 cup shredded part-skim mozzarella
    cheese
1/4 cup grated Parmesan cheese

Combine the cottage cheese, 2 cups mozzarella cheese and 1/2 cup Parmesan cheese in a bowl. Drain the spinach and squeeze dry. Add to the cheese mixture and mix well. Add the eggs and mix well.

Spread about 3/4 cup of the pasta sauce in a 9×13-inch baking dish. Alternate layers of 3 lasagna noodles, spinach mixture and sauce until all the ingredients are used, ending with sauce. Top with 1 cup mozzarella cheese and 1/4 cup Parmesan cheese. Bake at 350 degrees for 45 minutes. Let stand for 10 to 15 minutes before cutting.

YIELD: 6 TO 8 SERVINGS

Maple Syrup Chili

Not an ordinary chili. Skeptics quickly become believers.

2 to 3 cups chopped sweet onions
1 pound mushrooms, sliced
1 (28-ounce) can crushed tomatoes
1 (15-ounce) can red kidney beans
1 (15-ounce) can garbanzo beans
1 (15-ounce) can cannellini beans
1 (12-ounce) can tomato paste

$^3/_4$ cup maple syrup
1 cup raisins
1 tablespoon rice vinegar
1 tablespoon chili powder
1$^1/_2$ teaspoons dried basil
1 tablespoon crushed red pepper flakes
$^1/_4$ teaspoon cayenne pepper

Sauté the onions and mushrooms in a 6-quart soup pot until the onions are tender. Add the tomatoes. Rinse the beans in a colander under cold running water for 5 minutes, drain and add to the pot. Stir in the tomato paste, maple syrup, raisins, vinegar and seasonings. Simmer, covered, for 1 hour, stirring occasionally. Ladle into soup bowls. Garnish with shredded sharp Cheddar cheese, nonfat sour cream and unsalted cashews. Serve with corn muffins and salad.

YIELD: 8 SERVINGS

Vegetarian Chili

Taste as you cook—you'll want to adjust the seasonings to your taste.

Frozen vegetarian burger crumbles
1 (15-ounce) can kidney or black beans
1 teaspoon ground cumin
$^1/_2$ teaspoon chili powder
$^1/_2$ teaspoon turmeric

1 (16-ounce) can chopped tomatoes
Salt and pepper to taste
Shredded Cheddar cheese
Chopped onion

Add the desired amount of vegetarian crumbles to a saucepan and cook until heated through, stirring constantly. Add the beans, cumin, chili powder, turmeric and tomatoes and mix well. Heat to serving temperature and add salt and pepper. Ladle into soup bowls and top with shredded cheese and chopped onion. Serve with bread or crackers.

YIELD: 4 SERVINGS

BRUNCH AND BREADS

Seasons of the Heart Quilt
38" × 50"

Quilts often celebrate the holidays and seasons of the year. From Easter baskets in purples and yellows, to the red, white and blue banners of the Fourth of July, to the orange pumpkins of Halloween and the reds and greens of apple harvest and Christmas, the year marches along in living color. Artists capture the changing of the seasons with their paints and brushes. Quilters capture it with their fabrics and needle and thread.

Quilts celebrate the seasons of life, as well. Since the very early days of quiltmaking, quilts have been made to commemorate births, graduations, marriages, and anniversaries. These quilts—the history of a family stitched in fabric—have become treasured heirlooms, handed down from generation to generation.

Through their quilts, women have recorded the beauty and wonder of the seasons and the joys and memories of their lifetime.

BREAKFAST CASSEROLE

The beauty of this recipe is that almost any vegetable or meat works.

1 (8-count) can crescent rolls
1 medium onion, chopped
1 cup assorted chopped vegetables, such
   as cauliflower, broccoli and carrots
1 green bell pepper, chopped

1/2 (3-ounce) can bacon bits
2 cups shredded Cheddar cheese
4 eggs, slightly beaten
Salt and pepper to taste

Press the roll dough over the bottom of a 9×13-inch baking pan sprayed with nonstick cooking spray, sealing the edges and perforations. Spread a layer of the onion, assorted vegetables, green pepper and bacon bits over the roll dough. Sprinkle with the cheese.

Pour the eggs over the top, spreading to cover. Season with salt and pepper. Bake at 375 degrees for 20 minutes or until golden brown.

YIELD: 6 TO 8 SERVINGS

BRUNCH CASSEROLE

Best served with fresh fruit, Champagne and no conscience.

1 pound sliced bacon
1/4 cup (1/2 stick) butter
1/4 cup flour
2 cups milk, or 1 cup milk and
   1 cup cream
1/4 teaspoon thyme
1/4 teaspoon marjoram

1/4 teaspoon basil
4 cups shredded very sharp Cheddar
   cheese
12 hard-cooked eggs
1/4 cup finely chopped fresh parsley
Buttered bread crumbs

Cook the bacon in a large skillet until brown and crisp. Drain the bacon on paper towels; discard the drippings. Crumble the bacon and set aside. Melt the butter in a medium saucepan. Add the flour and blend well. Stir in the milk gradually. Cook over medium heat until smooth and thickened, stirring constantly. Stir in the thyme, marjoram and basil. Add the cheese gradually, stirring constantly until the cheese melts and the sauce is well blended. Remove from the heat and set aside. Peel the eggs carefully and cut into thin slices. Layer the egg slices, crumbled bacon, parsley and cheese sauce 1/3 at a time in a lightly greased 9×13-inch baking pan. Sprinkle the desired amount of the buttered bread crumbs over the top. Bake, uncovered, at 350 degrees for 30 minutes or golden brown.

YIELD: 8 SERVINGS

Mushroom Omelet

1 large onion, sliced
1 teaspoon sugar
1/4 cup extra-virgin olive oil
8 ounces fresh mushrooms, sliced
3 scallions, cut into 1-inch pieces
2 garlic cloves, minced

1 tablespoon red wine vinegar
8 eggs
1 tablespoon water
Salt and pepper to taste
4 or 5 sprigs flat-leaf parsley, chopped

Cook the onion with the sugar in the olive oil in a 9-inch ovenproof skillet over low heat for 30 minutes or until caramelized, stirring frequently. Add the mushrooms, scallions, garlic and vinegar and cook for 10 minutes longer. Remove half the mixture and set aside.

Whisk the eggs with the water, salt and pepper in a medium bowl. Increase the heat under the skillet to medium-low. Pour the egg mixture over the vegetables in the skillet. Tilt the skillet and lift the edge of the omelet gently to allow the uncooked egg to flow into the skillet. Cook until the eggs are almost set. Sprinkle the reserved mushroom mixture and the parsley over the egg mixture. Bake at 350 degrees for about 3 minutes.

YIELD: 3 OR 4 SERVINGS

Zucchini Oven Omelet

This omelet may also be prepared on the stovetop by melting a tablespoon of butter in a skillet over medium heat, adding the egg mixture and cooking, covered, for 10 to 15 minutes.

1 large onion, grated or finely chopped
1/4 cup (1/2 stick) butter
3 cups (1/4-inch) zucchini slices
1 teaspoon turmeric
1 teaspoon salt

1 teaspoon sugar
Pepper to taste
6 eggs
1 tablespoon vegetable oil

Cook the onion in the butter in a skillet over medium heat until transparent. Add the zucchini to the skillet and increase the heat to medium-high. Cook for 15 minutes or until the vegetables are light brown and the moisture has evaporated, stirring occasionally. Remove the skillet from the heat and mix in the turmeric, salt, sugar and pepper. Let stand until cool.

Beat the eggs in a large bowl with a wire whisk until frothy. Stir in the cooled zucchini mixture. Heat the vegetable oil in a nonstick baking pan or cake pan in a 350-degree oven. Pour the egg mixture into the prepared pan. Bake at 350 degrees for 30 minutes or until puffed and golden brown.

YIELD: 2 OR 3 SERVINGS

CAULIFLOWER QUICHE

This Israeli recipe is a favorite to serve during the festive holiday, Shavuoth,
when dairy-based meals are traditional.

½ to 1 small head cauliflower
½ cup crumbled bleu cheese
Quiche Crust
1 cup heavy cream
4 eggs

3 tablespoons flour
1 tablespoon dried tarragon
Salt and white pepper to taste
4 ounces shredded Muenster cheese

Remove the green leaves from the cauliflower and discard. Place the cauliflower in a large saucepan and cover with water. Bring the water to a boil and boil for 2 minutes. Remove from the heat and let the cauliflower stand in the hot water for 10 to 15 minutes. Drain well and let stand until cool. The cauliflower should be quite firm. Cut enough of the cauliflower into 1-inch pieces to measure 3 cups.

Sprinkle the bleu cheese over the unbaked Quiche Crust and arrange the cauliflower pieces over the cheese. Combine the cream, eggs, flour, tarragon, salt and pepper in a food processor and process until well blended. Pour the mixture over the cauliflower. Sprinkle the Muenster cheese over the top.

Bake at 350 degrees for 40 to 45 minutes or until a knife inserted in the center comes out clean. Let stand for several minutes before cutting into wedges.

YIELD: 8 TO 10 SERVINGS

QUICHE CRUST

1¼ cups flour
½ cup (1 stick) unsalted butter

1 egg
2 tablespoons cold water

Combine the flour, butter, egg and cold water in a food processor. Process until the mixture clings together to form a dough. Press the dough over the bottom and up the side of a 12- or 13-inch quiche dish.

Friendship is one of the greatest luxuries of life.
—*Edward Everett Hale*

CHEESE SOUFFLÉ STRATA

1 large loaf sourdough French bread
1/2 cup (1 stick) butter, softened
1 pound Cheddar cheese
4 eggs

2 1/2 cups milk
1 teaspoon dry mustard
1 teaspoon salt

Cut the bread into about 12 slices and remove the crusts. Spread the butter on both sides of each slice and cut into cubes. Cut the cheese into 1-inch cubes. Alternate layers of the bread cubes and cheese cubes in a 2-quart casserole sprayed with nonstick cooking spray.

Beat the eggs in a medium bowl. Add the milk, dry mustard and salt and beat until well blended. Pour the mixture over the layers.

Refrigerate, covered, for 5 hours to overnight. Bake, uncovered, at 350 degrees for 1 hour. Let stand for 5 minutes before serving.

YIELD: 6 SERVINGS

CHILES AND CHEESE CASSEROLE

*Serve this versatile dish for brunch, or as a side dish
with ham or roast beef.*

6 (4-ounce) cans whole green chiles
1 1/4 pounds Monterey Jack cheese, sliced
2 cups shredded Cheddar cheese
6 eggs

1 1/2 cups milk
5 tablespoons flour
1/2 teaspoon salt
Pepper to taste

Drain and rinse the green chiles under cold running water. Slit the chiles lengthwise to open and lay flat on paper towels to drain. Pat dry with paper towels. Layer the chiles, Monterey Jack cheese and Cheddar cheese 1/2 at a time in a greased 9×13-inch baking dish.

Beat the eggs in a medium bowl. Add the milk, flour, salt and pepper and beat until well blended. Pour over the layers. Bake at 350 degrees for 45 minutes or until set, puffy and golden brown.

YIELD: 12 SERVINGS

Ham and Asparagus Strata

The leftovers are delicious cold, but there probably won't be any.
Serve with fresh fruit for a wonderful brunch dish.

1 to 1½ pounds fresh asparagus, or
   2 (9-ounce) packages frozen
   asparagus cuts
1 loaf French bread (not sourdough)
Butter, softened
2 cups shredded Cheddar cheese

2 cups cubed cooked ham
8 eggs
4 cups half-and-half or milk
1 tablespoon dried onion flakes
1 teaspoon prepared grainy mustard
Salt and pepper to taste

Discard the tough ends of the asparagus and snap the spears into 1-inch pieces. Cook the asparagus in boiling water in a saucepan for 5 to 7 minutes or just until tender-crisp; drain well. (If using frozen asparagus, place the asparagus in a colander to drain while thawing.) Cut the bread into slices, trim off the crusts and butter the slices lightly on 1 side. Cut into 2-inch squares. Layer half the bread, half the cheese, all the ham and all the asparagus and the remaining bread in a greased 9×13-inch baking pan. Beat the eggs in a large bowl. Add about 1 cup of the half-and-half and beat until well blended. Beat in the remaining 3 cups half-and-half, onion flakes, mustard, salt and pepper. Pour the mixture over the layers. Sprinkle the remaining cheese over the top. Refrigerate, covered with foil, for 4 hours to overnight. Bake, uncovered, at 325 degrees for 1 hour or until set. Cover the edges with foil if the bread browns too quickly.

YIELD: 9 SERVINGS

Ham and Veggie Pies

2 cups chopped ham
1 cup shredded cheese
½ chopped bell pepper
½ cup chopped broccoli

4 eggs
2 cups milk
1 cup biscuit mix

Spray two 9-inch pie plates with nonstick cooking spray. Sprinkle half the ham, cheese, bell pepper and broccoli into each of the prepared pie plates and mix lightly. Combine the eggs, milk and biscuit mix in a bowl and beat until well blended. Divide the egg mixture between the pie plates. Bake at 400 degrees for 35 to 40 minutes or until set and lightly browned. Let stand for 5 minutes before cutting into wedges.

YIELD: 8 TO 12 SERVINGS

SAUSAGE BREAKFAST CASSEROLE

1 pound sausage
Butter, softened
12 slices bread, crusts trimmed
2 cups shredded sharp Cheddar cheese

4 eggs
2 cups milk
1/4 teaspoon salt
1/2 teaspoon pepper

Cook the sausage in a skillet until brown and crumbly, stirring frequently. Drain the sausage and set aside. Butter the bread slices on 1 side. Arrange half the bread with the buttered sides down in a 9×13-inch baking dish. Layer half the cheese, half the sausage, the remaining bread and the remaining cheese and sausage in the baking dish.

Beat the eggs in a medium mixing bowl. Add the milk, salt and pepper and beat until blended. Pour the egg mixture over the layers. Refrigerate, covered, overnight. Bake, uncovered, at 325 degrees for 40 minutes or until puffed and golden brown.

YIELD: 4 TO 6 SERVINGS

SAUSAGE STRATA

Make a low-fat version of this recipe by selecting 98 percent fat-free soup and turkey sausage or a sausage substitute. It is still delicious.

1 1/2 pounds sausage links
8 slices white bread, crusts trimmed
2 cups shredded sharp cheese
4 eggs
2 1/4 cups milk

3/4 teaspoon dry mustard
1 (10-ounce) can cream of
   mushroom soup
1/2 cup milk

Cook the sausage links in a skillet until brown on all sides, drain on paper towels and cut into pieces. Cut the bread into cubes. Layer the bread cubes, cheese and sausage in a 9×13-inch baking pan sprayed with nonstick cooking spray. Beat the eggs in a bowl. Add 2 1/4 cups milk and dry mustard and beat until well blended. Pour over the layers. Refrigerate, covered, overnight. Combine the soup and 1/2 cup milk in a bowl and mix well. Pour over the casserole. Bake at 275 degrees for 1 1/2 hours or until set and golden brown.

YIELD: 9 SERVINGS

Spinach Pie

8 ounces mild Italian sausage
2 (10-ounce) packages frozen chopped
   spinach
6 egg yolks
1½ cups shredded Cheddar, Swiss or
   Monterey Jack cheese
3 tablespoons minced dried onion

2 teaspoons Worcestershire sauce
Tabasco sauce to taste
6 egg whites
1 sheet puff pastry
1 egg
2 tablespoons water
Sesame seeds to taste

Remove the casing from the sausage and crumble the sausage into a skillet. Cook the sausage until brown and crumbly; drain well and set aside. Cook the spinach according to the package directions and drain well.

Combine the spinach, egg yolks, cheese, onion, sausage, Worcestershire sauce and Tabasco sauce in a bowl and mix well. Beat the egg whites in a mixing bowl until stiff peaks form. Fold the egg whites into the spinach mixture.

Pour the mixture into a greased 8-inch springform pan. Cut the puff pastry into strips and weave into a lattice over the spinach mixture. Beat the egg with the water and brush over the pastry lattice. Sprinkle with the sesame seeds.

Bake at 350 degrees for 30 minutes or until puffed and golden brown. Loosen from the side of the pan and remove the side of the pan. Cut into wedges.

YIELD: 6 SERVINGS

Zucchini Puff

*Omit the bacon for a vegetarian dish, serve hot or cold as a main course, or
cut into finger-size pieces to serve as an appetizer.*

12 ounces zucchini
1 large onion, finely chopped
3 slices bacon, finely chopped
4 ounces sharp cheese, finely shredded

1 cup self-rising flour
5 eggs, lightly beaten
½ cup vegetable oil

Grate the zucchini coarsely and drain well. Combine the zucchini, onion, bacon and cheese in a large bowl and toss to mix. Sprinkle the flour over the mixture and toss to mix. Beat the eggs and oil together, add to the zucchini mixture and mix well. Pour the mixture into a greased 8×12-inch baking pan. Bake at 375 degrees for 30 minutes or until a knife inserted in the center comes out clean.

YIELD: 6 SERVINGS

Zucchini and Sausage Supreme

2 pounds zucchini
8 ounces sausage
1/4 cup chopped onion
1/2 cup bread crumbs
1/2 cup grated Parmesan cheese

2 eggs, beaten
Thyme, rosemary and garlic to taste
Salt and pepper to taste
1/2 teaspoon MSG (optional)

Rinse the zucchini and trim the ends; do not peel. Slice the zucchini as desired and place in a saucepan. Add water to cover. Cook, covered, until tender, drain; mash and set aside.

Cook the sausage and onion in a skillet until brown and crumbly, stirring frequently; drain well and set aside. Toss the bread crumbs and cheese together and set aside. Combine the mashed zucchini, eggs and seasonings in a bowl and mix well. Reserve 1/3 of the bread crumb mixture. Add the remaining crumb mixture and the sausage to the zucchini mixture and mix well. Spoon the mixture into a greased 9-inch square baking pan. Sprinkle with the reserved crumb mixture. Bake at 350 degrees for 40 to 45 minutes or until golden brown.

YIELD: 4 TO 6 SERVINGS

Cheddar Chipped Beef

4 ounces fresh mushrooms, sliced
1 to 2 tablespoons butter
4 ounces chipped beef
2 tablespoons minced onion
1/2 cup (1 stick) butter

3 tablespoons flour
1 cup milk
1 cup sour cream
1 cup shredded Cheddar cheese

Sauté the mushrooms in 1 to 2 tablespoons butter in a skillet until tender and set aside. Cook the chipped beef and onion in 1/2 cup butter in a heavy skillet until the onion is tender. Sprinkle with the flour and stir in the milk. Cook until thickened, stirring constantly. Stir in the mushrooms, sour cream and cheese. Cook until the cheese melts, stirring constantly. Serve over toast points and garnish with chopped parsley.

YIELD: 1 OR 2 SERVINGS

The best antique is an old friend.

ROASTED CORN CUSTARD

6 to 8 ears fresh corn in the husk
1 onion, thinly sliced
2 tablespoons butter
3 eggs
1 cup heavy cream

$^1/_2$ cup milk
$^1/_2$ teaspoon nutmeg
Salt and freshly ground pepper to taste
2 tablespoons freshly chopped chives

Soak the unhusked corn in cold water to cover in a stockpot for 1 hour. Drain and place the corn on a medium-hot grill. Roast, covered, for 20 minutes or until tender, turning several times. Remove the husks, cut the kernels from the cobs and set aside. Cook the onion in the butter in a skillet over medium heat until tender and set aside.

Combine the eggs, cream, milk, nutmeg, salt and pepper in a large bowl and beat lightly. Add the corn and mix well. Pour the mixture into a buttered baking dish. Arrange the onion slices over the top. Bake at 350 degrees for 30 minutes or until set. Sprinkle the chives over the top.

YIELD: 6 TO 8 SERVINGS

ONION TART

$^3/_4$ cup (1$^1/_2$ sticks) unsalted butter
5 large Spanish or Vidalia onions, thinly
  sliced
Salt and pepper to taste

8 ounces puff pastry, thawed
1 tablespoon whole grain mustard
4 egg yolks
$^1/_3$ cup heavy cream

Melt the butter in a large skillet over low heat. Add the onions and stir gently to coat. Cook, covered, for 10 minutes. Uncover, increase the heat to medium-high and cook for 25 minutes or until the onions are tender and light golden brown, stirring occasionally. Sprinkle with salt and pepper and set aside to cool.

Roll the puff pastry to a $^1/_8$-inch thickness and fit into an 11-inch tart pan. Place foil over the pastry and place pie weights or dried beans evenly over the foil. Bake at 375 degrees for 25 minutes. Remove the foil with the weights.

Spread the mustard over the baked pastry. Beat the egg yolks with the cream in a large bowl. Add the onions and mix well. Pour the onion mixture into the tart shell. Bake at 375 degrees for 30 minutes or until set. Garnish with chopped chives and cut into wedges.

YIELD: 8 TO 12 SERVINGS

POTATO AND BACON PIE

Delicious served with a poached egg on each slice.

4 cups peeled cooked potatoes
1/2 cup milk

12 slices bacon, crisp-cooked, crumbled

Mash the potatoes in a large bowl but do not whip. Add the milk and mix well. Stir in the bacon. Spread the mixture evenly in a greased 8-inch pie plate. Bake at 350 degrees for 30 to 35 minutes or until lightly browned and crusty. Cut the pie into wedges.

YIELD: 6 SERVINGS

CHEESY POTATO CASSEROLE

2 pounds potatoes
1/4 cup (1/2 stick) butter or margarine,
    melted
1 small onion, chopped
1 teaspoon salt
1/4 teaspoon pepper
1 cup sour cream

1 (10-ounce) can cream of chicken soup
2 cups shredded Cheddar cheese
3 tablespoons butter or margarine, melted
1 1/2 cups herb-seasoned stuffing mix

Place the potatoes in a large saucepan with water to cover. Cook for 30 minutes or until tender. Drain and let stand until cool enough to handle. Peel the potatoes, cut into 1/4-inch strips. Combine 1/4 cup melted butter, onion, salt, pepper, sour cream and soup in a large bowl and mix well. Add the potatoes and the cheese and mix gently. Spoon the mixture into a lightly greased 9×13-inch baking dish.

Toss 3 tablespoons melted butter with the stuffing mix and sprinkle the mixture over the potato mixture. Bake at 350 degrees for 25 minutes or until heated through.

YIELD: 8 SERVINGS

The days that make us happy make us wise.

—John Masefield

Overnight Potato Bake

12 medium potatoes
8 ounces cream cheese, softened
1/2 cup (1 stick) butter, softened

1/2 cup sour cream
2 eggs, beaten
1/2 cup milk

Peel the potatoes, cut into cubes and place in a large saucepan. Add water to cover and cook until tender. Drain and mash the potatoes, adding the cream cheese and butter. Add the sour cream, eggs and milk and mix well; mixture will be thin. Pour the mixture into a buttered 2-quart baking dish. Refrigerate, covered, overnight. Bake at 350 degrees for 50 minutes or until lightly browned around the edges.

YIELD: 6 SERVINGS

Rolled Oat Biscuits

Try this filling, nutritious snack from Australia after school or with coffee.

1 1/3 cups packed brown sugar
1 cup (2 sticks) butter or margarine

2 2/3 cups rolled oats
1 1/3 cups shredded coconut

Grease an 8×11-inch baking pan and line with parchment paper. Combine the brown sugar and butter in a large saucepan over low heat. Heat until the margarine melts and the mixture is well blended, stirring occasionally. Remove from the heat. Add the oats and coconut and mix well.

Press the mixture evenly into the prepared baking pan. Bake at 325 degrees for 20 to 30 minutes; watch carefully as the brown sugar may caramelize and burn very quickly. Cut into 2×3-inch bars while hot.

YIELD: 16 SERVINGS

Refrigerator Butterhorns

1 envelope dry yeast
2 tablespoons (110- to 115-degree) warm
    water
2 cups (110- to 115-degree) warm milk
1/2 cup sugar
1 egg, beaten

1 teaspoon salt
6 cups flour
3/4 cup (1 1/2 sticks) butter or margarine,
    melted
Melted butter

Dissolve the yeast in the warm water in a large mixing bowl. Add the milk, sugar, egg, salt and 3 cups of the flour and mix well. Add 3/4 cup melted butter and the remaining 3 cups flour and beat until blended; do not knead. Place the dough in a greased bowl. Refrigerate, covered, overnight.

Punch the dough down and divide into 2 portions. Roll each portion into a 12-inch circle on a lightly floured surface. Cut each circle into 12 wedges. Roll up each wedge from the wide end and arrange with the points down 2 inches apart on a greased baking sheet. Let rise, loosely covered, in a warm place for 1 hour or until doubled in bulk. Bake at 350 degrees for 15 to 20 minutes or until golden brown. Brush the hot rolls with additional melted butter.

YIELD: 24 ROLLS

As for Rosemary I lette it runne all over
my garden walls, not onlie because my bees love it, but because
it is the herb sacred to remembrance and to friendship.

—*Sir Thomas More*

Banana Coconut White Chocolate Coffee Cake

2³/₄ cups flour
1¹/₄ teaspoons baking soda
1 teaspoon salt
1 cup (2 sticks) unsalted butter,
  softened
1 cup sugar
¹/₂ cup packed brown sugar

2 eggs
1 teaspoon vanilla extract
4 large ripe bananas, mashed
1 cup shredded coconut
1 cup white chocolate chips
White Chocolate Glaze

Sift the flour, baking soda and salt together and set aside. Cream the butter, sugar and brown sugar in a mixing bowl with an electric mixer at high speed until light and fluffy. Add the eggs 1 at a time and beat at low speed after each addition until well blended.

Add the vanilla and beat at medium speed for 5 minutes. Add the bananas and beat until smooth and well blended. Add the flour mixture gradually, beating constantly at low speed just until blended; do not overbeat.

Fold in the coconut and white chocolate chips. Pour the batter into a greased and floured 10-inch bundt pan and smooth the top of the batter. Bake at 350 degrees for 1 hour and 10 minutes or until the cake tests done.

Cool in the pan on a wire rack for 15 minutes. Invert onto a cake plate. Drizzle the White Chocolate Glaze over the cake.

YIELD: 12 TO 16 SERVINGS

White Chocolate Glaze

¹/₂ cup white chocolate chips
¹/₃ cup unsalted butter

1 tablespoon heavy cream

Combine the white chocolate chips, butter and cream in a small microwave-safe bowl or in a double boiler over hot water. Heat until the ingredients melt and whisk until smooth.

Poppy Seed Coffee Cake

Dust with confectioners' sugar just before serving for special occasions.

¹/₄ cup poppy seeds
1 cup buttermilk or sour milk
1 cup shortening
1¹/₂ cups sugar
4 eggs
1 teaspoon vanilla extract

2¹/₂ cups flour
¹/₂ teaspoon salt
1 teaspoon (rounded) baking soda
¹/₃ cup sugar
1 teaspoon cinnamon

Soak the poppy seeds in the buttermilk in a bowl for 2 hours or longer. Cream the shortening and 1¹/₂ cups sugar in a large mixing bowl until light and fluffy. Add the eggs and vanilla and beat until well blended.

Sift the flour, salt and baking soda together. Add the flour mixture and the poppy seed mixture to the creamed mixture alternately, beating well after each addition.

Combine ¹/₃ cup sugar and cinnamon in a small bowl and mix well. Pour ¹/₃ of the batter into a greased 12-cup bundt pan and sprinkle with ¹/₃ of the cinnamon-sugar. Repeat the layers 2 more times.

Bake at 350 degrees for 50 minutes or until the cake tests done. Cool in the pan on a wire rack for 15 minutes. Invert onto a cake plate.

YIELD: 12 TO 16 SERVINGS

That best portion of a good man's life—his little, nameless,
unremembered acts of kindness and of love.

—William Wordsworth

Strawberry Coffee Cake

8 ounces cream cheese, softened
1/2 cup (1 stick) butter or margarine,
   softened
3/4 cup sugar
1/4 cup milk
2 eggs, beaten
1 teaspoon vanilla extract

2 cups flour
1 teaspoon baking powder
1/2 teaspoon baking soda
1/4 teaspoon salt
1 (18-ounce) jar strawberry preserves
1/2 cup chopped walnuts
1/2 cup packed brown sugar

Combine the cream cheese, butter and sugar in a large mixing bowl and beat until light and fluffy. Add the milk, eggs and vanilla and mix well. Sift the flour, baking powder, baking soda and salt together. Add to the cream cheese mixture and beat until smooth. The batter will be very stiff.

Spread half the batter evenly in a greased and floured 9×13-inch baking pan. Spread the preserves over the batter. Add the remaining batter in dollops over the preserves. Sprinkle with the walnuts and brown sugar.

Bake at 350 degrees for 40 minutes. Cut into 3-inch squares and remove from the pan while hot. Serve warm or cool on a wire rack.

YIELD: 12 SERVINGS

Give what you have. To some one, it may be
better than you dare to think.

—*Henry Wadsworth Longfellow*

TEATIME DOUGHNUTS

1 egg
1/3 cup sugar
1/2 cup milk
1 tablespoon vegetable oil
1 1/2 cups flour

1/4 teaspoon salt
2 teaspoons baking powder
Vanilla extract or ground nutmeg to taste
Vegetable oil for deep frying
Confectioners' sugar or cinnamon-sugar

Beat the egg in a medium bowl until frothy. Add the sugar, milk and 1 tablespoon oil and beat until blended. Sift the flour, salt and baking powder together. Add to the egg mixture along with vanilla or nutmeg, beating until smooth. Preheat the oil for deep frying in a large heavy skillet or deep fryer. Drop the batter by teaspoonfuls into the hot oil. Deep-fry until brown on both sides, turning once. Drain on paper towels. Roll in confectioners' sugar or cinnamon-sugar to coat. The doughnuts will be about the size of a large walnut.

YIELD: 6 TO 8 SERVINGS

RAISIN SCONES

1 cup raisins
2 1/2 cups flour
1/2 cup sugar
1 teaspoon cream of tartar
1 teaspoon baking soda

1/2 teaspoon salt
1/2 cup shortening
1 egg
1 cup sour cream

Plump the raisins in water to cover in a small bowl for several minutes; drain well and set aside. Sift the flour, sugar, cream of tartar, baking soda and salt into a large bowl. Cut in the shortening until crumbly. Beat the egg in a small bowl and reserve a small amount for the glaze. Blend the sour cream into the remaining egg. Add the plumped raisins and the sour cream mixture to the flour mixture and mix well. Pat the dough to 3/4-inch thickness on a lightly floured surface and cut into 8 diamonds. Arrange the diamonds on an ungreased baking sheet and brush with the reserved beaten egg. Bake at 425 degrees for 12 minutes or until golden brown. Serve warm or cool on a wire rack.

YIELD: 8 SCONES

Broccoli Corn Bread

1 (10-ounce) package frozen chopped
  broccoli or spinach, thawed
1 (8-ounce) package corn bread mix
3 eggs, beaten
1 medium onion, chopped
1 cup shredded sharp Cheddar cheese

1/2 cup (1 stick) butter or margarine,
  melted
1/2 teaspoon salt
1/4 to 1/2 teaspoon garlic salt
1/4 teaspoon ground red pepper, or
  5 or 6 drops hot sauce

Drain the broccoli and press between paper towels. Combine the corn bread mix, eggs, onion, cheese, melted butter, salt, garlic salt and red pepper in a large bowl and mix well. Stir in the broccoli; the batter will be thick.

Heat a 10-inch cast iron skillet sprayed with nonstick cooking spray in a 375-degree oven. Pour the batter into the hot skillet. Bake at 375 degrees for 25 to 30 minutes or until golden brown. Cool slightly before cutting into wedges.

YIELD: 8 SERVINGS

Southern Corn Bread

1 1/2 cups cornmeal
1/2 cup flour
1/4 cup sugar
1/2 teaspoon baking soda
1 egg, beaten

1/3 cup vegetable oil
1 1/2 cups buttermilk
1 cup fresh or unsalted canned whole
  kernel corn, drained

Mix the cornmeal, flour, sugar and baking soda in a bowl. Beat the egg in a medium bowl. Add the oil and buttermilk and mix well. Stir in the corn. Stir in the cornmeal mixture. Pour the batter into a greased 8-inch square baking pan. Bake at 425 degrees for 20 to 25 minutes or until golden brown and a wooden pick inserted in the center comes out clean.

YIELD: 6 TO 8 SERVINGS

Friendship is the golden thread that
ties all hearts together.

CHEESE BREAD

1 loaf Italian bread
1 cup (2 sticks) butter, softened
2 tablespoons dried minced onion
1 tablespoon prepared mustard

2 teaspoons lemon juice
1/2 teaspoon seasoned salt
1 tablespoon poppy seeds
8 ounces Swiss cheese, sliced

Cut the loaf into slices, cutting to but not through the bottom. Combine the butter, dried onion, mustard, lemon juice, seasoned salt and poppy seeds in a bowl and mix until well blended.

Spread the butter mixture over the cut surfaces of the bread. Insert cheese slices between the bread slices. Wrap the loaf in foil. Bake at 350 degrees for 45 minutes.

YIELD: 12 SERVINGS

HERBED GARLIC BREAD

Better make two loaves—one never seems to be enough.

1 (1-pound) oval loaf French or
    sourdough bread
3/4 cup (1 1/2 sticks) unsalted butter,
    softened
1/4 cup finely chopped fresh parsley
1/4 cup finely chopped fresh chives or
    green onion tops

1/2 teaspoon salt
1/2 teaspoon dried basil
1/2 teaspoon dried thyme
2 medium garlic cloves, crushed
3 tablespoons grated Parmesan cheese

Trim the crust from the top and sides of the bread. Cut into 2-inch diagonal slices, cutting to but not through the bottom. Cut 2-inch diagonal slices in the opposite direction to form triangles.

Combine the butter, parsley, chives, salt, basil, thyme and garlic in a mixing bowl or food processor and mix until well mixed and spreadable. Spread the mixture between the cuts and over the top and sides of the loaf.

Place on a baking sheet and sprinkle with Parmesan cheese. Bake at 400 degrees for 15 to 20 minutes or until golden brown. May wrap in foil and refrigerate or freeze. Place on a baking sheet and bring to room temperature before adding the cheese and baking.

YIELD: 6 SERVINGS

CRANBERRY APPLE BREAD

1¹/₂ cups flour
1¹/₂ teaspoons baking powder
1 teaspoon cinnamon
¹/₂ teaspoon baking soda
2 cups chopped peeled Golden Delicious
   apples

³/₄ cup sugar
2 tablespoons vegetable oil
¹/₄ cup egg substitute
1 cup chopped cranberries
¹/₂ cup chopped walnuts or pecans

Combine the flour, baking powder, cinnamon and baking soda in a bowl and mix well. Combine the apples, sugar and oil in a separate bowl and mix well. Add the egg substitute and mix well. Add the flour mixture and stir just until moistened. Stir in the cranberries and walnuts; the batter will be thick. Pour the batter into a greased 4×8-inch loaf pan. Bake at 350 degrees for 1 hour or until a wooden pick inserted in the center comes out clean. Turn the loaf onto a wire rack to cool.

YIELD: 1 LOAF (6 SERVINGS)

DATE BREAD

1 pound pitted dates
2 teaspoons baking soda
2 cups boiling water
2 tablespoons butter, softened
1¹/₂ cups sugar

2 teaspoons vanilla extract
2 eggs
3¹/₂ cups flour
2 teaspoons baking powder

Chop the dates and place in a medium bowl. Add the baking soda and boiling water, mix well and set aside to cool.

Beat the butter and sugar in a mixing bowl until light and fluffy. Add the vanilla and eggs and beat until well blended. Add the cooled date mixture and mix well. Mix the flour and baking powder together. Add to the date mixture and mix well. Pour the batter into 2 greased 5×9-inch loaf pans.

Bake at 350 degrees for 45 minutes or until a wooden pick inserted in the center comes out clean. Turn the loaves onto wire racks to cool.

YIELD: 2 LOAVES (12 SERVINGS)

Irish Country Bread

This "every day" loaf came from Ireland in the 1800s.

3/4 cup sugar
1 egg
2 tablespoons melted butter
1 1/2 cups flour
1 1/2 teaspoons baking powder
1/4 teaspoon salt

3/4 cup milk
1/2 cup chopped walnuts
1/2 cup raisins (optional)
1 tablespoon sugar
1/4 teaspoon cinnamon

Combine 3/4 cup sugar, egg and melted butter in a large mixing bowl and mix well. Combine the flour, baking powder and salt and mix well. Add the milk and flour mixture to the egg mixture alternately, mixing well after each addition. Fold in the walnuts and raisins. Pour the batter into a greased and floured loaf pan. Mix 1 tablespoon sugar and the cinnamon together and sprinkle over the batter.

Bake at 350 degrees for 35 to 40 minutes or until golden brown and a wooden pick inserted in the center comes out clean. Turn the loaf onto a wire rack to cool.

YIELD: 1 LOAF (10 TO 12 SERVINGS)

Irish Soda Bread

This bread is both authentic and delicious.

4 cups sifted flour
1 tablespoon baking soda
1 tablespoon sugar
2 1/2 teaspoons salt
1/4 teaspoon cream of tartar

1 1/2 cups dark raisins (optional)
2 tablespoons caraway seeds (optional)
1 1/2 to 2 cups buttermilk
1 to 2 tablespoons melted butter

Combine the flour, baking soda, sugar, salt and cream of tartar in a large mixing bowl and mix well. Add the raisins and caraway seeds and mix well. Add enough buttermilk to make a dough, mixing with a fork until the ingredients are moistened.

Turn the dough onto a lightly floured surface and knead for 1 to 2 minutes or until well mixed. Shape the dough into a large ball and place on a well greased baking sheet. Flatten the dough into a 7-inch circle and cut an X that is 1/4 inch deep in the center of the circle.

Bake at 375 degrees for 35 to 40 minutes or until the top is golden brown and the loaf sounds hollow when rapped with knuckles. Remove the loaf to a wire rack and brush with the melted butter. Let stand until completely cooled before slicing.

YIELD: 1 LOAF (12 SERVINGS)

Poppy Seed Bread

3 eggs
2¹/₄ cups sugar
1¹/₂ cups vegetable oil
1¹/₂ cups milk
2 teaspoons almond extract

3 cups flour
1¹/₂ teaspoons baking powder
¹/₂ teaspoons salt
1¹/₂ tablespoons poppy seeds

Beat the eggs lightly in a large mixing bowl. Add the sugar and mix well. Add the oil, milk and almond extract and mix well. Combine the flour, baking powder and salt. Add to the egg mixture and beat until well blended. Add the poppy seeds and mix well. The batter will be thin. Divide the batter between 2 greased and floured 4×8-inch loaf pans.

Bake at 350 degrees for 1 hour or until a wooden pick inserted in the center comes out clean. Cool the loaves in the pans on a wire rack for 10 minutes. Loosen the loaves from the sides of the pans and turn onto wire racks. Let stand until completely cooled. Wrap in plastic wrap and store at room temperature.

YIELD: 2 LOAVES (12 SERVINGS)

Pumpkin Bread

This bread can do double duty—it goes well with stew and chili and can also be served as a dessert-type bread.

4 cups flour
2 teaspoons baking soda
1 teaspoon baking powder
1¹/₂ teaspoons salt
1 teaspoon nutmeg
1 teaspoon cinnamon
1 teaspoon allspice
¹/₂ teaspoon cloves

3 cups sugar
1 cup vegetable oil
1 (16-ounce) can pumpkin
²/₃ cup cold water
4 eggs
1 cup chopped nuts
1 cup raisins

Sift the flour, baking soda, baking powder, salt, nutmeg, cinnamon, allspice and cloves into a large mixing bowl. Add the sugar and mix well. Make a well in the center of the mixture. Pour the oil, pumpkin and water into the well and beat until well blended. Add the eggs 1 at a time, beating well after each addition. Add the nuts and raisins and stir until well mixed. Divide the batter among 3 well greased 5×9-inch loaf pans.

Bake at 350 degrees for 1 hour or until a wooden pick inserted in the center comes out clean. Turn the loaves onto wire racks to cool.

YIELD: 3 LOAVES (24 SERVINGS)

CRANBERRY PUMPKIN BREAD

4 eggs
2/3 cup water
1 cup vegetable oil
1 (16-ounce) can pumpkin
3 cups whole wheat flour or 3 1/2 cups
   all-purpose flour
2 cups sugar

2 teaspoons baking soda
1 1/2 teaspoons salt
1 teaspoon cinnamon
1 teaspoon nutmeg
1/8 teaspoon ground cloves
2 cups whole or chopped cranberries

Beat the eggs in a large mixing bowl. Add the water, oil and pumpkin and mix until well blended. Sift the flour, sugar, baking soda, salt, cinnamon, nutmeg and cloves together. Add the flour mixture to the egg mixture gradually, mixing until the batter is well blended. Stir in the cranberries. Divide the batter among 3 well greased 4×8-inch loaf pans.

    Bake at 350 degrees for 1 hour or until a wooden pick inserted in the center comes out clean. Let the bread cool in the pans on wire racks.

YIELD: 3 LOAVES (18 SERVINGS)

KENTUCKY PUMPKIN BREAD-IN-A-JAR

Did you know that vegetables and fruits are only some of the foods that can be "canned?"
These make great gifts. Add a ribbon and your own label.

2 2/3 cups sugar
2/3 cup shortening
4 eggs
2 cups pumpkin
3 1/2 cups flour
2 teaspoons baking soda

1/2 teaspoon baking powder
1 teaspoon cinnamon
1 teaspoon ground cloves
2/3 cup water
2/3 cup chocolate chips

Grease 8 straight-sided, wide-mouth 1-pint canning jars and set aside. Cream the sugar and shortening in a large mixing bowl until light and fluffy. Add the eggs and pumpkin and beat until well blended. Sift the flour, baking soda, baking powder, cinnamon and cloves together. Add the flour mixture and water alternately to the pumpkin mixture, mixing well after each addition. Stir in the chocolate chips.

    Fill the jars half full. Arrange the jars on a baking sheet; do not allow the jars to touch. Bake at 325 degrees for 45 minutes.

    Remove the jars from the oven and seal with two-piece lids. Let the jars stand to cool. In a few minutes you will hear "pops" as the bread cools and the lids seal airtight.

YIELD: 8 JARS (32 SERVINGS)

STRAWBERRY BREAD

3 cups flour
2 cups sugar
1 teaspoon baking soda
1 teaspoon cinnamon
1 teaspoon salt

4 eggs
1 cup vegetable oil
2 (10-ounce) packages frozen strawberries,
    thawed

Combine the flour, sugar, baking soda, cinnamon and salt in a bowl and mix well. Beat the eggs in a mixing bowl. Add the oil and strawberries and mix well. Stir the flour mixture into the strawberry mixture gradually and mix well. Pour the batter into 2 greased loaf pans. Bake at 350 degrees for 55 to 65 minutes or until a wooden pick inserted in the center comes out clean. Cool the loaves in the pans on wire racks for 15 minutes. Turn the loaves onto wire racks to cool completely. Serve with strawberry cream cheese.

YIELD: 2 LOAVES (12 SERVINGS)

PINEAPPLE ZUCCHINI BREAD

3 eggs
2 cups sugar
1 cup vegetable oil
2 teaspoons vanilla extract
2 cups shredded zucchini
1 (8-ounce) can crushed pineapple,
    drained

3 cups flour
2 teaspoons baking soda
1 teaspoon salt
1/2 teaspoon baking powder
1 1/2 teaspoons cinnamon
3/4 teaspoon nutmeg
1 cup chopped walnuts

Beat the eggs lightly in a large mixing bowl. Add the sugar, oil and vanilla and beat until the mixture is thick and frothy. Add the zucchini and pineapple and mix well. Sift the flour, baking soda, salt, baking powder, cinnamon and nutmeg together and stir into the zucchini mixture, mixing well. Stir in the walnuts. Divide the batter between 2 greased and floured 5×9-inch loaf pans. Bake at 350 degrees for 1 hour or until a wooden pick inserted in the center comes out clean. Cool in the pans on a wire rack for several minutes. Turn onto wire racks to cool completely. This bread freezes well.

YIELD: 2 LOAVES (18 SERVINGS)

Apple and Yogurt Muffins

You won't believe this moist, tasty muffin has only 2 grams of fat.

4 cups chopped peeled Granny Smith
    apples
1 cup sugar
1 egg
1 egg white
1/2 cup nonfat plain yogurt
2 teaspoons vanilla extract

2 cups flour
2 teaspoons baking soda
2 teaspoons cinnamon
1 teaspoon salt
1 cup raisins
1/4 cup chopped walnuts

Combine the apples and sugar in a large bowl, toss lightly to coat and set aside. Combine the egg, egg white, yogurt and vanilla in a small mixing bowl and beat until smooth. Add to the apple mixture and mix well. Combine the flour, baking soda, cinnamon and salt and mix well.

Sprinkle the flour mixture over the apple mixture and stir until well mixed. Stir in the raisins and walnuts. Spoon the batter into greased muffin cups. Bake at 325 degrees for 20 to 25 minutes or until golden brown.

YIELD: 16 MUFFINS

Blueberry Muffins

1 cup sugar
1/2 (1 stick) butter, softened
2 eggs
1 teaspoon vanilla extract
2 cups flour

2 teaspoons baking powder
1/2 teaspoon salt
1/2 cup milk
2 cups blueberries

Preheat the oven to 450 degrees. Cream the sugar and butter in a mixing bowl until light and fluffy. Add the eggs and vanilla and beat until well blended. Mix the flour, baking powder and salt together. Add to the egg mixture and mix well. Stir in the milk and fold in the blueberries. Spoon into paper-lined muffin cups.

Place the muffin pans in the preheated oven and reduce the oven temperature to 375 degrees. Bake for 35 minutes or until golden brown.

YIELD: 12 MUFFINS

BRAN MUFFINS

The batter may be stored in a sealed container in the refrigerator and baked as needed. If you wish to bake fewer muffins than the number of cups in the pan, simply add water to the empty cups. The steam will make the muffins moister.

2¹/₂ cups flour
1 teaspoon salt
2¹/₂ teaspoons baking soda
2 cups digestive bran
1 cup chopped dried fruit

1 cup flaked coconut
2 eggs
1 cup packed brown sugar
¹/₂ cup safflower oil
2 cups milk

Sift the flour, salt, baking soda and bran together. Add the fruit and coconut and mix well. Beat the eggs in a large mixing bowl until thick and pale yellow. Add the brown sugar gradually, beating constantly. Add the safflower oil, beating constantly. Add the flour mixture to the egg mixture alternately with the milk, mixing well after each addition. Fill greased muffin cups ²/₃ full. Bake at 350 degrees for 15 to 20 minutes or until golden brown and a wooden pick inserted in the center comes out clean. Editor's Note: If you plan to refrigerate the batter, use egg substitute equivalent to the eggs. Digestive bran is available in many health food stores.

YIELD: 36 MUFFINS

CRANBERRY MUFFINS WITH HOT BUTTER SAUCE

1 cup sugar
3 tablespoons butter, softened
¹/₂ cup evaporated milk
¹/₂ cup water
2 cups flour
1 teaspoon salt

2 teaspoons baking soda
2 cups cranberry halves
2 cups sugar
1 cup (2 sticks) butter
1 cup evaporated milk
2 teaspoons vanilla extract

Cream 1 cup sugar and 3 tablespoons butter in a mixing bowl until light and fluffy. Add ¹/₂ cup evaporated milk and water and beat until well blended. Mix the flour, salt and baking soda together. Add the flour mixture to the sugar mixture and mix well. Stir in the cranberries. Spoon the batter into greased muffin cups. Bake at 350 degrees for 30 minutes or until golden brown.

Combine 2 cups sugar, 1 cup butter and 1 cup evaporated milk in a saucepan. Bring to a boil, stirring until well blended. Remove from the heat and stir in the vanilla. Serve over the muffins.

YIELD: 12 TO 15 MUFFINS

GERMAN BLACK FOREST MUFFINS

Fabulous hybrid of basic muffins and a traditional Black Forest cake from Germany.

1 cup unbleached flour
1 cup whole wheat flour
2 teaspoons baking powder
1/2 teaspoon baking soda
3 tablespoons baking cocoa
1/2 cup ground almonds

1 egg
3/4 cup packed brown sugar
1 cup buttermilk
1/3 cup safflower oil
2 tablespoons brandy
1 1/2 cups drained cherries

Combine the flours, baking powder, baking soda, baking cocoa and almonds in a bowl, mix well and set aside. Whisk the egg in a large mixing bowl. Add the brown sugar, buttermilk, oil and brandy and whisk until well blended. Add the cherries and mix well. Add the mixed dry ingredients and stir for 10 to 20 seconds or just until moistened. Spoon into greased muffin cups.

Bake at 375 degrees for 25 minutes or until a wooden pick inserted in the center comes out clean. Serve the muffins warm with whipped cream.

YIELD: 12 MUFFINS

MINCEMEAT MUFFINS

1 egg
6 tablespoons canola oil
6 tablespoons sugar
2 tablespoons brown sugar
1 cup milk
2/3 cup mincemeat

2/3 cup natural bran
1 cup plus 2 tablespoons flour
1 teaspoon baking powder
1 teaspoon baking soda
1/2 teaspoon salt

Beat the egg and canola oil in a mixing bowl until well blended. Add the sugar and brown sugar and beat until well mixed. Add the milk and mincemeat and mix well.

Stir in the bran and let stand for 10 minutes. Mix the flour, baking powder, baking soda and salt together. Add to the bran mixture and stir until well mixed. Spoon into greased muffin cups.

Bake at 375 degrees for 18 to 20 minutes or until a wooden pick inserted in the center comes out clean.

YIELD: 12 MUFFINS

SWEET POTATO AND PECAN MUFFINS

6 tablespoons butter, softened
$2/3$ cup sugar
1 egg
1 teaspoon vanilla extract
$1^3/4$ cups flour

$1^1/2$ teaspoons baking powder
$1/2$ teaspoon salt
$2/3$ cup milk
1 sweet potato, peeled, finely grated
$2/3$ cup chopped pecans

Cream the butter and sugar in a large mixing bowl until light and fluffy. Add the egg and vanilla and beat until blended. Mix the flour, baking powder and salt together. Add the flour mixture to the creamed mixture alternately with the milk, beating just until moistened after each addition. Fold in the sweet potato and pecans. Spoon the batter into 6 greased muffin cups. Bake at 375 degrees for 25 to 30 minutes or until golden brown.

YIELD: 6 MUFFINS

BUTTERMILK FRENCH TOAST

8 eggs
$1^1/4$ cups buttermilk
$1^1/4$ teaspoons vanilla extract
Salt to taste

Butter
14 thick slices white bread
Cinnamon to taste
Confectioners' sugar

Combine the eggs, buttermilk, vanilla and salt in a large bowl and beat with a fork until blended. Melt a small amount of butter on a hot griddle or skillet over medium-high heat. Dip the bread slices 1 at a time into the egg mixture and place in the butter. Spoon a bit of the egg mixture onto the slice and sprinkle with cinnamon. Fry until brown on both sides, turning once. Place the toast on serving plates and sprinkle generously with confectioners' sugar. Garnish with fresh strawberries.

YIELD: 14 SERVINGS

A task worth doing and friends worth
having make life worthwhile.

Baked Apple Pancake

*This recipe was found in a kitchen drawer in a mountain cabin
and the date on it was 1932.*

2 tablespoons butter
3 tablespoons sugar
1 tablespoon cinnamon
1 large apple, cored, sliced
4 eggs

2/3 cup milk
1/3 cup flour
1 tablespoon sugar
1/2 teaspoon salt

Melt the butter in a 10-inch ovenproof skillet. Mix 3 tablespoons sugar with the cinnamon.
Sprinkle the cinnamon-sugar evenly in the skillet and arrange the apple slices decoratively.
Cook over medium heat for 3 to 4 minutes. Let stand until slightly cooled.

Beat the eggs in a mixing bowl. Add the milk, flour, 1 tablespoon sugar and salt and beat
until smooth. Pour the batter carefully over the apple slices.

Bake at 400 degrees for 15 to 20 minutes or until golden brown and puffy around the
edges. Serve immediately.

YIELD: 2 TO 4 SERVINGS

Puffy Baked Pancake

1 cup flour
1 tablespoon sugar
1/4 teaspoon salt
1 1/4 cups milk

2 eggs, beaten
1 tablespoon unsalted butter
Confectioners' sugar

Combine the flour, sugar and salt in a large mixing bowl. Add the milk and eggs and mix until
blended. Melt the butter in a shallow baking pan. Pour the batter into the melted butter. Bake
at 375 degrees for 30 minutes or until puffed and golden brown. Dust generously with
confectioners' sugar and serve with fresh fruit.

YIELD: 6 SERVINGS

THE ULTIMATE PANCAKE

For the ultimate experience, top each serving with a fried egg.

2 cups rice flour
1 cup milk
2 eggs, beaten
1/2 cup mashed banana
4 teaspoons baking powder

Butter
3 cups plain nonfat yogurt
Apple and Pear Sauce
Toasted Sunflower Seeds

Combine the rice flour, milk, eggs, banana and baking powder in a large bowl and mix well. Add a small amount of water to make the batter of a medium-thin consistency. Preheat a griddle over medium-low heat. Butter the griddle, pour enough of the batter onto the griddle to make pancakes of the desired size and bake until golden brown on both sides, turning once. Repeat with the remaining batter. Stack the pancakes for individual servings, spreading a thick layer of the yogurt between the pancakes. Ladle hot Apple and Pear Sauce over the top and sprinkle with the Toasted Sunflower Seeds.

YIELD: 8 SERVINGS

APPLE AND PEAR SAUCE

2 apples, cut into bite-size pieces
2 pears, cut into bite-size pieces
1/8 teaspoon cinnamon

1/8 teaspoon nutmeg
1/8 teaspoon allspice
1 1/4 cups maple syrup

Combine the apples, pears and spices in a saucepan over medium heat. Cook until the fruit pieces are tender but still hold their shape. Add the maple syrup and cook for 5 minutes longer, stirring occasionally.

TOASTED SUNFLOWER SEEDS

3/4 cup sunflower kernels

1 teaspoon olive oil

Combine the sunflower seeds and olive oil in a small skillet over medium heat. Heat until the kernels are toasted, stirring occasionally.

Blueberry Belgian Waffles

Try replacing the blueberries with chopped apples or strawberries. Serve any flavor waffles with vanilla ice cream, or just serve with real maple syrup!

2 eggs, beaten
2¹/₄ cups milk
¹/₂ cup vegetable oil
2¹/₄ cups flour

4 teaspoons baking powder
³/₄ teaspoon salt
1¹/₂ tablespoons sugar
1 to 2 cups fresh or frozen blueberries

Combine the eggs, milk and oil in a large bowl and blend well. Combine the flour, baking powder, salt and sugar and mix well. Add the blueberries to the flour mixture and mix gently. Add the blueberry mixture to the egg mixture all at once and mix just until moistened. Bake the batter in a preheated waffle iron or Belgian waffle iron according to the manufacturer's instructions.

YIELD: 10 WAFFLES

Sticky Buns

¹/₂ cup chopped pecans
¹/₂ cup raisins
1 (24-count) package frozen roll dough
1 (4-ounce) package butterscotch pudding
 mix (not instant)

¹/₂ cup (1 stick) butter
³/₄ cup packed brown sugar
1 teaspoon cinnamon

Grease a 9×13-inch baking pan. Sprinkle the pecans and raisins in the prepared pan and arrange the frozen rolls in the pan. Sprinkle the dry pudding mix over the frozen rolls.

Combine the butter, brown sugar and cinnamon in a saucepan. Bring to a boil over medium heat. Drizzle the mixture over the rolls. Cover the pan tightly with foil.

Let the pan stand at room temperature overnight to rise. Remove the foil and bake at 350 degrees for 30 minutes or until golden brown. Invert the hot rolls onto a baking sheet and serve immediately.

YIELD: 12 SERVINGS

PHILADELPHIA DANISH

This recipe is perfect for busy quilters—it's simple and fast, but your friends and family will never realize you slaved over quarter-inch seams, not an oven.

2 (8-count) cans crescent rolls
16 ounces cream cheese, softened
1 cup sugar
1 tablespoon vanilla extract

1 egg yolk
1 egg white
Confectioners' sugar or fruit topping

Unroll 1 can of the roll dough and fit the dough into the bottom of a 9×13-inch baking pan, sealing the edges and perforations.

Combine the cream cheese, sugar, vanilla and egg yolk in a mixing bowl and beat until smooth and creamy. Spread evenly over the roll dough.

Unroll the second can of roll dough. Place the dough over the cream cheese layer, sealing the edges and perforations. Beat the egg white lightly in a small bowl and brush over the roll dough.

Bake at 350 degrees for 20 to 30 minutes or until golden brown. Sprinkle with confectioners' sugar or top with a favorite fruit topping.

YIELD: 15 SERVINGS

I find friendship to be like wine, raw when new, ripened with age,
the true old man's milk and restorative cordial.

—Thomas Jefferson

VEGETABLES AND SIDE DISHES

Hopeful Hearts Quilt
22" × 28"

The colors of springtime are the colors of hope, promise, and youth. Quilts in pretty pastel hues of pink, blue, yellow, and green are used to welcome the arrival of a sweet new baby, and yummy shades of raspberry, lemon, and lime sherbet often decorate a little girl's bedroom.

It's no wonder that the women of the 1930s turned to this happy springtime palette for their quilts. During the Great Depression, when money was scarce and pleasures few, people found ways to escape the worries of the day. On Saturday afternoon they forgot their troubles as Shirley Temple tap-danced across the silver screen and into their hearts. It was the days of the Hollywood musical where everyone lived happily ever after. It was also the time of a quilt revival in the country. Quilting gave women an economical means of providing bedding for their families, but it also gave them a much-needed creative diversion and a chance to bring beauty into their lives. The pretty pastel quilts of the '30s are radiant with sunny optimism and the hope for a brighter tomorrow.

CALICO BEANS

1 pound ground beef or sausage, or
    8 ounces of each
$1/2$ to 1 pound sliced bacon
1 large onion, sliced
1 (16-ounce) can lima beans
1 (16-ounce) can kidney beans
1 (16-ounce) can pinto beans
1 (16-ounce) can red beans
1 (16-ounce) can garbanzo beans
1 (16-ounce) can black beans

1 (16-ounce) can pork and beans
$1/2$ cup packed brown sugar
1 cup ketchup
$1/4$ cup vinegar
$1/4$ cup molasses
1 tablespoon prepared mustard
$1/2$ teaspoon horseradish
$1/2$ teaspoon Worcestershire sauce
$1/2$ teaspoon seasoned salt
$1/2$ teaspoon pepper

Cook the ground beef, bacon and onion in a large skillet, stirring until beef is brown and crumbly and drain well. Drain all the beans except the pork and beans. Combine all the beans with the ground beef mixture in a slow cooker, baking pan or microwave-safe baking dish. Add the brown sugar, ketchup, vinegar, molasses, mustard, horseradish, Worcestershire sauce, seasoned salt and pepper and mix well.

    Cook in a slow cooker on High for 3 to 4 hours or on Low overnight; or bake at 300 degrees for 2 hours or until bubbly; or microwave on High until hot and bubbly, stirring every 5 minutes. The flavors blend best when slow-cooked overnight.

    YIELD: 16 TO 20 SERVINGS

BEANS RAREBIT

4 slices bacon
1 large onion, chopped
1 (28-ounce) can pork and beans
1 (16-ounce) can red kidney beans
1 (16-ounce) can lima beans

$1/3$ cup ketchup
$1/2$ cup packed brown sugar
1 teaspoon Worcestershire sauce
4 ounces sharp cheese, cubed

Chop the bacon and fry in a large skillet until crisp. Remove the bacon and set aside. Add the onion to the skillet and sauté in the drippings until tender. Drain all the beans. Combine the sautéed onion, bacon, beans, ketchup, brown sugar, Worcestershire sauce and cheese in a 2-quart baking dish and mix well. Bake, covered, at 350 degrees for 1 hour.

    YIELD: 6 TO 8 SERVINGS

Broccoli Puff

1 1/2 pounds fresh broccoli, chopped
2 (10-ounce) cans cream of
   mushroom soup
2 cups shredded Cheddar cheese
1/2 cup milk

1/2 cup mayonnaise
2 eggs, beaten
1 cup fine dry bread crumbs
1/4 cup (1/2 stick) butter, melted

Boil the broccoli in water to cover in a saucepan until tender-crisp and drain well. Arrange the broccoli in a shallow layer in a greased 9×13-inch baking dish. Combine the soup and cheese in a bowl and mix well. Add the milk, mayonnaise and eggs and mix well. Spoon the mixture over the broccoli. Toss the bread crumbs and butter together and sprinkle over the top. Bake at 400 degrees for 25 minutes or until lightly browned.

YIELD: 8 SERVINGS

Broccoli Hollandaise

*Turn this vegetable side dish into a luncheon treat by adding a
layer of sliced or chopped ham.*

12 slices bread
8 slices American cheese
2 (10-ounce) packages frozen chopped
   broccoli

6 eggs, beaten
3 cups milk
2 tablespoons dried onion flakes
1 teaspoon dry mustard

Trim the crusts from the bread and discard. Cut circles from the centers of the bread slices with a biscuit cutter and reserve the circles and trimmings. Arrange the bread trimmings in a greased 9×13-inch baking dish and arrange the cheese slices over the bread. Cook the broccoli according to the package directions and drain well. Spread the broccoli over the cheese and arrange the bread circles on top of the broccoli.

Combine the eggs, milk, onion flakes and dry mustard in a blender and process until well mixed. Pour the mixture over the layers. Refrigerate, covered with foil, for 8 hours to overnight. Bake, uncovered, at 350 degrees for 1 hour or until set.

YIELD: 12 SERVINGS

Sweet-and-Sour Red Cabbage

1 large onion, chopped
1 tablespoon butter
1¼ pounds red cabbage, cored, chopped
1 apple, peeled, chopped

½ teaspoon salt
2 tablespoons brown sugar
2 tablespoons cider vinegar
1 cup water

Sauté the onion in the butter in a large skillet for 1 minute. Add the cabbage and apple and sauté for 5 minutes. Combine the salt, brown sugar, cider vinegar and water in a small bowl and mix well. Stir the mixture into the cabbage mixture and simmer, covered, for 30 minutes. Serve hot or cold.

YIELD: 6 SERVINGS

Shaker Baked Carrots

Add ½ cup of any leftover baked carrots to 3 cups hot cooked rice, kasha or barley for an interesting and colorful pilaf.

3 cups grated carrots
1 teaspoon salt
½ teaspoon pepper

1 teaspoon ground ginger
1 tablespoon brown sugar
3 tablespoons butter, melted

Combine the carrots, salt, pepper, ginger and brown sugar in a baking dish and toss lightly to mix. Drizzle the butter over the carrot mixture. Bake, covered, at 350 degrees for 30 minutes.

YIELD: 6 SERVINGS

Wishing to be friends is quick work, but friendship
is a slow-ripening fruit.

—*Aristotle*

CARROT CASSEROLE

Even people who don't like carrots love this—must be the sauce.

12 large carrots, thinly sliced
1/2 cup (1 stick) margarine
1/4 cup flour
1 teaspoon salt
1/4 teaspoon celery salt
1/4 teaspoon pepper

1/2 teaspoon dry mustard
1 small onion, chopped
2 cups milk
8 ounces Velveeta cheese, sliced
Buttered bread crumbs or crushed
   potato chips

Cook the carrots in a small amount of water in a covered saucepan until tender and drain well. Melt the margarine in a saucepan over medium heat. Add the flour, salt, celery salt, pepper and dry mustard and blend well. Add the onion and cook for several minutes, stirring constantly. Stir in the milk gradually and cook until thickened, stirring constantly. Layer half the carrots, all the cheese and the remaining carrots in a large greased casserole. Spoon the sauce over the layers; do not stir. Sprinkle the crumbs over the top. Bake at 325 degrees for 30 minutes or until bubbly.

YIELD: 8 TO 12 SERVINGS

CORN PUDDING

This recipe was brought to the United States from England in the late 1800s.

2 1/2 cups fresh or canned whole
   kernel corn
2 tablespoons flour
1 tablespoon sugar
1 1/2 tablespoons butter, melted

1 teaspoon salt
1/4 teaspoon pepper
2 eggs, lightly beaten
1 1/2 cups milk

Prepare the fresh corn by cutting the kernels from the cobs with a sharp knife and then scraping the cobs with the back of the knife to obtain the remaining corn pulp. Place the corn in a large bowl and add the flour, sugar, butter, salt and pepper and mix well. Whisk the eggs with the milk until well blended. Pour the egg mixture into the corn mixture and mix well. Pour the mixture into a well greased 1 1/2-quart baking dish. Place the dish in a larger baking pan. Add hot water to half the depth of the pan. Bake at 350 degrees for 60 to 70 minutes or until a knife inserted in the center comes out clean.

YIELD: 6 TO 8 SERVINGS

CORN CASSEROLE

2 (16-ounce) cans cream-style corn
2 (7-ounce) packages Mexican
   corn bread mix
3 eggs, beaten

1 medium onion, chopped
1/2 cup vegetable oil
2 cups shredded Cheddar cheese

Combine the corn, corn bread mix, eggs, onion and oil in a large bowl and mix well. Add the cheese and mix well. Spoon the mixture into a greased 9×13-inch baking dish. Bake at 350 degrees for 45 minutes or until set and golden brown.

YIELD: 12 SERVINGS

VIDALIA ONION CASSEROLE

5 or 6 Vidalia onions
1/2 cup (1 stick) butter
3/4 cup butter cracker crumbs
3/4 cup crushed cheese crackers
1 cup shredded Cheddar cheese

1 (10-ounce) can cream of
   mushroom soup
Grated Parmesan cheese and paprika
   to taste

Slice the onions as desired. Sauté the onions in the butter in a large skillet for several minutes. Mix the butter cracker and cheese cracker crumbs together. Alternate layers of the sautéed onions, cracker crumbs and Cheddar cheese 1/3 at a time in a greased 9×13-inch baking dish. Spread the soup over the top and sprinkle with the desired amounts of Parmesan cheese and paprika. Bake at 350 degrees for 30 minutes.

YIELD: 8 TO 10 SERVINGS

OVEN CHIP ROASTIES

4 medium to large baking potatoes
2/3 cup (about) olive oil

1 teaspoon mixed herbs
Salt to taste

Heat a lightly oiled large roasting pan in a 450-degree oven. Cut the potatoes into thin wedges. Brush the wedges on all sides with the olive oil and place in a single layer in the roasting pan. Sprinkle with herbs and salt. Bake at 450 degrees for 20 minutes or until crisp, golden brown and puffy. Serve immediately.

YIELD: 4 TO 6 SERVINGS

Snowy Mashed Potato Casserole

4 pounds potatoes
Salt to taste
8 ounces cream cheese, softened
1 cup sour cream
2 teaspoons salt

1/8 teaspoon pepper
1 garlic clove, crushed
1/4 cup chopped chives
1 teaspoon paprika
1 tablespoon butter

Peel and chop the potatoes. Cook in salted water to cover in a large saucepan until tender. Drain the potatoes and place in a large mixing bowl and mash. Add the cream cheese, sour cream, 2 teaspoons salt, pepper and garlic and beat until smooth. Stir in the chives. Spoon the mixture into a buttered 9×13-inch baking dish. Sprinkle with the paprika and dot with the butter. Bake at 350 degrees for 30 minutes.

YIELD: 10 TO 12 SERVINGS

Comforting Scalloped Potatoes

*Nutmeg is a traditional Greek addition to béchamel sauce in moussaka,
and adds a familiar but unique flavor to this dish.*

6 medium potatoes
2 teaspoons salt
1/3 cup butter or margarine
1/3 cup flour
1 1/3 cups 2% milk

1/3 cup reduced-fat sour cream
1/2 teaspoon nutmeg
Salt to taste
1/3 cup (or more) shredded Cheddar
 cheese

Peel the potatoes and cut into 1/4-inch slices. Place in a 2-quart saucepan and add 2 teaspoons salt and water to cover. Boil until almost tender and drain well. Melt the butter in a heavy saucepan. Add the flour and blend well. Cook for several minutes, stirring constantly to form a roux. Stir in the milk gradually. Cook until thickened, stirring constantly. Remove from the heat and stir in the sour cream, nutmeg and salt to taste.

Combine the sauce and the potatoes in a large bowl and mix gently to coat. Spoon the potato mixture into a buttered 2-quart casserole and top with the cheese. Bake at 350 degrees for 30 minutes or microwave on Medium-High for 10 minutes.

YIELD: 8 SERVINGS

Holiday Potato Dish

8 medium potatoes
1 cup chopped onion
1/4 cup (1/2 stick) butter
1 (10-ounce) can cream of
    mushroom soup

2 cups sour cream
1 1/2 cups shredded cheese
Salt and pepper to taste
1/2 cup crushed cornflakes
3 tablespoons butter, melted

Cook the potatoes in boiling water to cover in a large saucepan until tender. Drain the potatoes, cool and peel. Shred the potatoes and place in a large mixing bowl. Sauté the onion in 1/4 cup butter in a skillet until tender. Remove from the heat and stir in the soup and sour cream. Add the cheese and the onion mixture to the potatoes and mix well. Season with salt and pepper and spoon the potato mixture into a greased 9×13-inch baking dish.

Refrigerate, covered, overnight. Sprinkle the cornflakes over the top and drizzle with 3 tablespoons melted butter. Bake at 350 degrees for 1 1/2 hours.

YIELD: 8 SERVINGS

Swiss Potatoes

6 medium potatoes
Salt and pepper to taste
6 medium onions
1/2 cup milk

1/2 cup dry white wine
8 ounces Swiss cheese, sliced
1/2 to 1 cup dry white wine

Peel the potatoes and slice very thinly. Layer the potato slices in a greased 9×13-inch baking dish, sprinkling each layer with salt and pepper. Slice the onions very thinly and cut the slices into halves. Arrange the onion slices over the potatoes. Pour the milk and 1/2 cup wine over the layers. Arrange Swiss cheese slices over the top in an overlapping layer. Bake, covered with foil, at 350 degrees for 45 minutes. Remove the foil and add 1/2 to 1 cup wine. Bake, uncovered, for 15 minutes longer.

YIELD: 6 SERVINGS

When making dinner for a friend, don't forget the love.
—*Jeanne Moreau*

ARABIAN SPINACH

1 onion, sliced
2 tablespoons olive oil or sunflower oil
2 garlic cloves, crushed
1 teaspoon cumin seeds

14 ounces fresh spinach
1 (15-ounce) can garbanzo beans
2 tablespoons butter
Salt and pepper to taste

Sauté the onion in the olive oil in a large skillet for 5 minutes or until tender. Add the garlic and cumin seeds and cook for 1 minute longer. Rinse the spinach, pat dry and cut into shreds. Add the spinach to the skillet gradually, stirring until the spinach wilts. Add the garbanzo beans, butter, salt and pepper. Heat just until the mixture bubbles and serve immediately. May pour off pan juices before serving if desired.

YIELD: 4 SERVINGS

SPINACH WITH RAISINS AND PINE NUTS

This is a version of a classic Roman dish that dates back thousands of years. The pine nuts and raisins are an interesting addition to the flavor and texture of the spinach.

2 tablespoons raisins
2 (10-ounce) packages fresh spinach
1 garlic clove, minced

1/4 cup olive oil
3 tablespoons pine nuts
Salt to taste

Soak the raisins in boiling water to cover for 15 minutes. Drain well, squeeze dry and set aside. Rinse the spinach well, discard the stems and pat dry. Sauté the garlic in the olive oil in a large skillet for 2 to 3 minutes or until brown but not burned. Add the raisins and pine nuts and sauté for about 1 minute or until the pine nuts are brown. Add half the spinach and cook for about 3 minutes or just until the spinach is cooked, tossing constantly. Remove the spinach mixture to a serving dish with a slotted spoon. Add the remaining spinach to the skillet and cook for about 3 minutes, tossing constantly. Add to the serving dish and toss to mix. Season with salt and serve immediately.

YIELD: 6 SERVINGS

Friendship is the breathing rose, with sweets in every fold.

—*Oliver Wendell Holmes*

SQUASH STUFF

2 pounds yellow squash or zucchini
1 cup mayonnaise
1 cup grated Parmesan cheese
1 small onion, finely chopped
2 eggs, beaten

1/2 teaspoon salt
1/4 teaspoon pepper
1/2 cup soft bread crumbs
1 tablespoon margarine, melted

Slice the squash and cook in a small amount of water in a saucepan for 10 to 15 minutes or until tender. Drain the squash and let stand until slightly cooled. Combine the mayonnaise, cheese, onion, eggs, salt and pepper in a large bowl and mix well. Add the squash and mix gently. Spoon the mixture into a lightly greased 1 1/2-quart casserole. Toss the bread crumbs with the margarine and sprinkle over the squash mixture. Bake at 350 degrees for 30 minutes.

YIELD: 6 SERVINGS

GREEN TOMATO CASSEROLE

1/4 cup chopped onion
1 cup dry bread crumbs
1 teaspoon Italian seasoning
2 teaspoons parsley flakes

1/2 teaspoon salt
Pepper to taste
6 medium green tomatoes
2 tablespoons grated Parmesan cheese

Microwave the onion in a microwave-safe bowl on High for 2 minutes. Add the bread crumbs, Italian seasoning, parsley flakes, salt and pepper and toss to mix well. Cut the green tomatoes into 1/2-inch slices. Alternate layers of the green tomato slices and crumb mixture 1/2 at a time in a greased 2-quart casserole. Sprinkle the cheese over the top. Bake at 350 degrees for 30 to 45 minutes or until the tomatoes are tender and the top is brown.

YIELD: 6 SERVINGS

True friends, like ivy and the wall
Both stand together, and together fall.

—*Thomas Carlyle*

TURNIP CASSEROLE

6 cups chopped turnips
1/4 cup fine bread crumbs
1/4 cup cream
1/2 teaspoon salt

1/4 teaspoon pepper
3/4 to 1 teaspoon ground ginger
2 eggs, beaten
3 tablespoons butter, melted

Cook the turnips in water to cover in a saucepan until tender, drain well and mash until smooth. Combine the bread crumbs and cream in a large bowl and let stand for several minutes. Add the salt, pepper, ginger and eggs and mix well. Add the mashed turnips and mix well. Spoon the mixture into a greased 2 1/2-quart casserole. Drizzle the butter over the top. Bake at 350 degrees for 1 hour or until light brown.

YIELD: 6 TO 8 SERVINGS

ZUCCHINI AND CARROTS WITH HERB STUFFING

6 cups chopped zucchini
1/4 cup chopped onion
3/4 cup water
Salt to taste
1 (10-ounce) can cream of
chicken soup

1 cup sour cream
1 cup shredded carrots
1/2 cup (1 stick) butter or margarine
1 (8-ounce) package herb-seasoned
stuffing mix

Cook the zucchini and onion in the water with salt to taste for 5 minutes, drain and set aside. Combine the soup, sour cream and carrots in a large bowl and mix well. Add the zucchini mixture and mix well. Melt the butter in a large skillet. Add the stuffing mix and toss until the stuffing is well mixed with the butter. Spread 1/2 of the stuffing mixture in a greased 8×11-inch baking dish. Spoon the zucchini mixture over the stuffing and cover with the remaining stuffing mixture. Bake at 350 degrees for 25 to 30 minutes or until brown.

YIELD: 8 SERVINGS

Have a heart that never hardens, and a temper that never
tires, and a touch that never hurts.

—*Charles Dickens*

Garden Vegetable Casserole

3 large potatoes
1 large zucchini
4 or 5 small tomatoes
3 large carrots

1 cup chicken bouillon
1 to 2 cups seasoned croutons
1/4 cup (1/2 stick) margarine, melted
2 cups shredded Cheddar cheese

Peel the potatoes, slice thinly and place in a greased 2 1/2-quart casserole. Cut the zucchini into small chunks and layer over the potatoes. Cut the tomatoes into chunks and layer over the zucchini. Slice the carrots thinly and add to the casserole. Pour the bouillon over the layers. Bake, covered, at 375 degrees for 1 hour. Toss the croutons with the margarine and spread over the vegetables. Sprinkle the cheese over the top. Bake for 15 minutes longer or until the cheese is melted and brown.

YIELD: 6 TO 8 SERVINGS

Vegetable Couscous

1 (10-ounce) package couscous
2 cups chopped fresh tomatoes
1 (15-ounce) can garbanzo beans
1/2 cup chopped green bell pepper
1/2 cup chopped green onions

1 tablespoon chopped fresh oregano
1 teaspoon paprika
1 teaspoon olive oil
1 garlic clove, minced
1/4 cup grated Parmesan cheese

Cook the couscous according to the package directions and set aside to keep hot. Combine the tomatoes, undrained garbanzo beans, green pepper, green onions, oregano, paprika, olive oil and garlic in a large saucepan. Bring to a boil, stirring frequently. Spoon the couscous into a serving bowl. Ladle the vegetable mixture over the couscous. Sprinkle the cheese over the top.

YIELD: 6 SERVINGS

Love is sharing a part of yourself with others.

CRANBERRY RELISH

1 (16-ounce) can whole cranberry sauce
1 (8-ounce) can crushed pineapple
1 cup red grapes

1 orange, peeled, chopped
1/3 to 1/2 cup chopped walnuts or pecans

Pour the cranberry sauce into a large bowl and mash lightly with a fork. Drain the pineapple and add to the bowl. Seed the grapes, cut into quarters and add to the cranberry mixture. Add the orange pieces and walnuts and mix lightly. Chill, covered, overnight.

YIELD: 6 TO 8 SERVINGS

SPICED CRANBERRIES

2 or 3 cinnamon sticks
1 teaspoon whole cloves
2 cups sugar
1/2 bottle port

1/2 cup orange juice
1 teaspoon grated orange peel
4 cups cranberries

Tie the cinnamon and cloves in cheesecloth. Combine the sugar, port, orange juice, orange peel and the spice bag in a saucepan. Bring to a boil, stirring until the sugar dissolves completely. Reduce the heat and simmer for 5 minutes. Add the cranberries. Simmer until the cranberries pop; do not stir. Remove the spice bag and discard. Skim off the foam. Pour the cranberry mixture into a bowl. Chill, covered, before serving.

YIELD: 3 TO 4 CUPS

We can do no great things—only small things with great love.

—*Mother Teresa*

BAKED GREEN RICE

3 cups hot cooked rice
2 cups shredded Monterey Jack or mild
   Cheddar cheese
1/3 cup butter or margarine
1 (4-ounce) can chopped green chiles,
   drained

1 cup finely chopped dried parsley
1 small onion, chopped
2 eggs, beaten
1 cup milk
1 teaspoon salt
1/4 teaspoon pepper

Combine the rice with the cheese and butter in a large mixing bowl and toss until well mixed. Add the green chiles, parsley, onion, eggs, milk, salt and pepper and mix well. Spoon the mixture into a greased 2-quart baking dish. Bake, covered, at 350 degrees for 30 minutes. Bake, uncovered, for 10 minutes longer.

YIELD: 8 SERVINGS

SPINACH AND RICE

1 (10-ounce) package fresh spinach
1/3 cup uncooked rice
4 scallions
1/2 teaspoon onion salt

Salt and pepper to taste
1/3 cup olive oil or canola oil
1/4 cup water

Rinse the spinach and drain well. Press the spinach into a 3-quart baking dish. Layer the rice over the spinach. Cut the scallions into 1/2-inch pieces and layer over the rice. Sprinkle with the seasonings and shake the casserole to allow the rice to settle into the spinach. Drizzle the olive oil and water over the top. Bake, covered, at 350 degrees for 40 to 50 minutes or until the rice is tender, stirring occasionally and adding small amounts of water if necessary.

YIELD: 4 SERVINGS

We attract hearts by the qualities we display; we retain them
by the qualities we possess.

—*Jean Baptiste Antoine Suard*

Pine Nut and Orange Wild Rice

3 cups water
1 cup wild rice
2 cups water
1 cup brown rice
1 cup dried currants or golden raisins
$^1/_2$ cup toasted pine nuts
$^1/_4$ cup chopped fresh parsley

2 tablespoons grated orange peel
$^1/_4$ cup olive oil
2 to 3 tablespoons freshly squeezed
    orange juice
Salt and freshly ground pepper to taste
Freshly grated Parmesan cheese to taste

Bring 3 cups water to a boil in a large saucepan and stir in the wild rice. Reduce the heat and simmer, covered, for 25 to 45 minutes or until the wild rice is tender. Drain if necessary, place the rice in a large bowl and set aside. Bring 2 cups water to a boil in a medium saucepan and stir in the brown rice. Reduce the heat and simmer, covered, for 25 minutes or until tender. Add to the wild rice in the bowl and toss to mix. Combine the currants, pine nuts, parsley, orange peel, olive oil, orange juice and salt and pepper in a small bowl and toss until well mixed. Add to the rice mixture and toss to mix. Spoon into a lightly greased baking dish. Bake, covered, at 350 degrees for 20 minutes or until heated through. Sprinkle with Parmesan cheese before serving.

YIELD: 8 SERVINGS

Wild Rice Patties

1 (6-ounce) package long grain and wild
    rice mix
3 eggs, beaten
1 cup chopped nuts
$^1/_2$ cup mayonnaise

1 small onion, chopped
Vegetable oil for frying
1 (10-ounce) can cream of
    mushroom soup
Milk

Cook the rice mix according to the package directions, pour into a mixing bowl and let stand until slightly cooled. Add the eggs, nuts, mayonnaise and onion and mix well. Shape into patties of the desired size and place on waxed paper. Heat a small amount of oil in a large heavy skillet. Add the rice patties and cook until brown on both sides, turning once. Drain on paper towels. Heat the soup with enough milk in a saucepan to make a sauce of the desired consistency. Serve the rice patties with the mushroom sauce.

YIELD: 6 SERVINGS

RICE AND MUSHROOMS

*If you wish to prepare this dish in advance, combine the "dry" ingredients in a
baking dish and add the "liquids" just before baking.*

2²/3 cups quick-cooking rice
6 tablespoons vegetable oil
2 (4-ounce) cans mushrooms, drained
5 or 6 green onions with tops, chopped

2 (10-ounce) cans beef consommé
2 tablespoons soy sauce
1/2 teaspoon salt

Combine the uncooked rice, oil, mushrooms, green onions, consommé, soy sauce and salt in a
large bowl and mix well. Spoon into a greased baking dish. Bake, covered, at 350 degrees for
30 to 45 minutes or just until the liquid is absorbed; do not stir while baking.

YIELD: 6 SERVINGS

SPANISH RICE

1¹/2 cups uncooked rice
3 cups water
1 pound link sausage
1 large onion, chopped
1 green bell pepper, chopped
1 to 2 tablespoons butter
4 cups chopped canned tomatoes

1 cup salsa
2 teaspoons chili powder
2 teaspoons garlic powder
1 teaspoon salt
1 teaspoon pepper
Tabasco sauce to taste

Cook the rice in the water in a saucepan according to the package directions and set aside.
Cook the sausage in boiling water to cover until cooked through. Drain the sausage and cut
into pieces. Sauté the onion and green pepper in the butter in a skillet until tender.

Combine the cooked rice, sausage pieces, sautéed vegetables, tomatoes, salsa, chili
powder, garlic powder, salt, pepper and Tabasco sauce in a large bowl and mix well. Spoon into
a greased 9×13-inch baking dish. Bake, covered, at 350 degrees for 1 hour.

YIELD: 6 SERVINGS

DESSERTS, CAKES AND PIES

Homespun Hearts Quilt
40" × 40"

Wishing to recapture a simpler, quieter time, many of us decorate our homes with quilts. As a symbol of the past, they add an inviting, country look to warm our bodies and soothe our souls.

No fabrics typify the country life more than homespun plaids and stripes—a nostalgic reminder of the days when fabrics were woven by hand to clothe the family and provide warm bedding. Women sat with their families at evening time and created quilts from their scrap bags, stitching simple traditional designs handed down from family members and passed from neighbor to neighbor. Homespun folk-art quilts continue to represent that less-hurried time when life was centered around home and family and the simple pleasures of life.

OREO CHEESECAKE

32 ounces cream cheese, softened
1¼ cups sugar
2 tablespoons flour
4 eggs, at room temperature
3 egg yolks, at room temperature

⅓ cup heavy cream
1 teaspoon vanilla extract
15 Oreo cookies
Oreo Crust
Sour Cream Topping

Beat the cream cheese in a mixing bowl with an electric mixer at medium speed until smooth and creamy. Add the sugar gradually, beating constantly. Beat for 3 minutes or until light and fluffy. Beat in the flour. Add the eggs and egg yolks and beat until smooth. Beat in the cream and vanilla. Chop the cookies to yield about 1½ cups pieces. Pour half the cream cheese mixture into the Oreo Crust, sprinkle with the chopped cookies and add the remaining cream cheese mixture.

Place the springform pan on a baking sheet. Bake at 425 degrees for 15 minutes. Reduce the oven temperature to 225 degrees and bake for 50 minutes longer or until set. Remove the cheesecake from the oven. Increase the oven temperature to 350 degrees. Spread the Sour Cream Topping evenly over the cream cheese layer. Bake for 7 minutes. Remove to a wire rack and let stand until cooled to room temperature.

Refrigerate, covered, for several hours to 3 days. Loosen the cheesecake from the side of the pan and remove the side of the pan. Place on a serving plate. Garnish with whole Oreo cookies.

YIELD: 10 TO 12 SERVINGS

OREO CRUST

25 Oreo cookies

¼ cup (½ stick) unsalted butter, melted

Process the cookies in a food processor until crushed to about 2½ cups crumbs. Add the melted butter and process until well mixed. Press evenly over the bottom and ⅔ of the way up the side of a 9- or 10-inch springform pan. Refrigerate while preparing the filling.

SOUR CREAM TOPPING

2 cups sour cream
¼ cup sugar

1 teaspoon vanilla extract

Combine the sour cream, sugar and vanilla in a small bowl and blend well.

Pumpkin Cheesecake

24 ounces cream cheese, softened
3/4 cup sugar
3/4 cup packed brown sugar
5 eggs
1/4 cup heavy cream
1 teaspoon cinnamon

1/2 teaspoon nutmeg
1/4 teaspoon ground cloves
2 3/4 cups (heaping) canned pumpkin
Vanilla Wafer Crust
Walnut Topping

Combine the cream cheese, sugar and brown sugar in a large mixing bowl and beat until light and fluffy. Add the eggs 1 at a time, beating well after each addition. Add the cream, cinnamon, nutmeg, cloves and pumpkin and blend well. Pour into the Vanilla Wafer Crust.

Place the springform pan on a baking sheet or place a foil-lined baking sheet in the bottom of the oven to catch any drips. Bake at 350 degrees for 1 hour. Spoon the Walnut Topping over the top of the cheesecake. Bake for 20 to 25 minutes longer or until a knife inserted in the center comes out clean.

Let stand until completely cooled. Chill for 3 hours to overnight. Loosen the cheesecake from the side of the pan and remove the side of the pan.

YIELD: 10 SERVINGS

Vanilla Wafer Crust

1 3/4 cups vanilla wafer crumbs
1/2 cup sugar

7 tablespoons butter, melted

Combine the crumbs, sugar and butter in a bowl and mix well. Press the mixture over the bottom and up the side of a lightly greased 9-inch springform pan.

Walnut Topping

6 tablespoons butter, softened
1 cup packed brown sugar

1 cup chopped walnuts

Cream the butter and brown sugar in a mixing bowl until light and fluffy. Add the walnuts and mix well.

SOUR CREAM CHEESECAKE

2¹/₂ cups graham cracker crumbs
¹/₄ cup sugar
¹/₂ cup (1 stick) butter or margarine,
    softened
40 ounces cream cheese, softened
1³/₄ cups sugar
3 tablespoons flour

1 tablespoon grated lemon peel
¹/₄ teaspoon vanilla extract
5 eggs
2 egg yolks
¹/₄ cup heavy cream
¹/₂ cup sour cream

Combine the graham cracker crumbs, ¹/₄ cup sugar and butter in a medium bowl and mix until the mixture holds together. Press the crumb mixture over the bottom and up the side of a 9-inch springform pan. Chill while preparing the filling. Combine the cream cheese, 1³/₄ cups sugar, flour, lemon peel and vanilla in a large mixing bowl and beat with an electric mixer at high speed just until blended. Add the eggs and egg yolks 1 at a time, beating well after each addition. Add the cream and beat just until blended. Pour the cream cheese mixture into the prepared springform pan. Bake at 500 degrees for 10 minutes. Reduce the oven temperature to 250 degrees and bake for 1 hour longer. Spread the sour cream over the top. Let the cheesecake cool on a wire rack. Refrigerate for 3 hours to overnight. Loosen the cheesecake from the side of the pan and remove the side of the pan. Cut into wedges. Serve plain or with strawberries.

YIELD: 16 TO 20 SERVINGS

SOUR CREAM APPLE SQUARES

2 cups flour
2 cups packed brown sugar
¹/₂ cup (1 stick) margarine, softened
1 cup chopped walnuts
2 teaspoons cinnamon
1 teaspoon baking soda

¹/₂ teaspoon salt
1 cup sour cream
1 teaspoon vanilla extract
1 egg, beaten
2 cups chopped peeled apples

Combine the flour, brown sugar and margarine in a mixing bowl and beat with an electric mixer at low speed until crumbly. Stir in the walnuts. Press about 2³/₄ cups of the mixture over the bottom of an ungreased 9×13-inch baking pan. Add the cinnamon, baking soda, salt, sour cream, vanilla and egg to the remaining mixture in the bowl and beat until well mixed. Stir in the apples. Spoon the apple mixture into the prepared pan. Bake at 350 degrees for 35 to 40 minutes or until the apples are tender and the top is golden brown. Cool on a wire rack. Cut into squares and serve with whipped cream.

YIELD: 12 TO 15 SERVINGS

FROSTED APPLE BARS

2¹/₂ cups flour
1 teaspoon salt
1 cup shortening
1 egg yolk
¹/₂ cup (about) milk
1 cup crushed cornflakes
3 tablespoons cornstarch
2 teaspoons cinnamon

1 (12-ounce) can frozen apple juice
    concentrate, thawed
12 cups sliced peeled apples
1 tablespoon margarine
1 egg white, beaten
1 cup confectioners' sugar
1 tablespoon water
1 teaspoon vanilla extract

Mix the flour and salt in a bowl. Cut in the shortening. Beat the egg yolk in a 1-cup measure. Add enough milk to measure ²/₃ cup. Add to the flour mixture and mix with a fork just until the mixture clings together. Shape the dough into a ball. Divide into 2 portions. Roll 1 portion into a large rectangle on a lightly floured surface. Fit the dough into the bottom and up the sides of a 10×15-inch baking pan. Sprinkle with the cornflake crumbs. Blend the cornstarch, cinnamon and apple juice concentrate in a saucepan. Cook over medium heat until thickened, stirring constantly. Combine with the apple slices in a large bowl. Spread mixture evenly in the pastry-lined pan and dot with the margarine. Cover with the remaining dough, sealing the edges and cutting vents. Brush with the egg white. Bake at 375 degrees for 1 hour. Blend the remaining ingredients in a bowl. Spread over the warm layer. Cut into bars.

YIELD: 1¹/₂ TO 2 DOZEN

BLUEBERRY BUCKLE

1¹/₂ cups sugar
¹/₂ cup (1 stick) butter, softened
2 eggs
4 cups flour
4 teaspoons baking powder
1 teaspoon salt

1 cup milk
4 cups drained blueberries
1 cup sugar
²/₃ cup flour
1 teaspoon cinnamon
¹/₂ cup (1 stick) butter

Beat 1¹/₂ cups sugar and ¹/₂ cup softened butter in a mixing bowl until light and fluffy. Add the eggs and beat until blended. Mix 4 cups flour, baking powder and salt together. Add the flour mixture to the egg mixture alternately with the milk, mixing well after each addition. Fold in the blueberries. Spoon into a greased 9×13-inch baking dish. Combine 1 cup sugar, ²/₃ cup flour and cinnamon in a small bowl and mix well. Cut in ¹/₂ cup butter until the mixture is crumbly. Sprinkle over the top. Bake at 375 degrees for 45 to 50 minutes. Serve warm or at room temperature; plain or with ice cream or whipped cream.

YIELD: 12 SERVINGS

FRESH PEACH COBBLER

Fresh or frozen peach slices
3 tablespoons butter, melted
1/2 cup (or more) milk
3/4 cup sugar
1 cup flour

1 teaspoon baking powder
1/4 teaspoon salt
3/4 cup sugar
1 tablespoon cornstarch
1 cup water

Place a generous layer of peach slices in a 9×13-inch baking pan (if using frozen peach slices, place the peaches in the pan and allow to thaw). Mix the butter and milk in a bowl. Add 3/4 cup sugar, flour, baking powder and salt and mix until smooth. The batter should be thin enough to pour; add additional milk 1 tablespoon at a time as necessary.

Pour the batter over the peaches; it is not necessary to cover the peaches entirely. Combine 3/4 cup sugar, cornstarch and water in a small bowl and mix well. Pour the mixture over the batter. Bake at 350 degrees for 45 minutes. Broil for about 2 minutes if a brown top is desired but watch carefully to avoid overbrowning. Serve warm with vanilla ice cream.

YIELD: 6 SERVINGS

RHUBARB CRISP

1 cup packed brown sugar
1 cup flour
3/4 cup quick-cooking oats
1/2 cup (1 stick) margarine, melted
3 cups finely chopped rhubarb

1 cup sugar
2 tablespoons cornstarch
1 cup water
1 teaspoon vanilla extract
4 drops red food coloring (optional)

Mix the brown sugar, flour and oats in a bowl. Stir in the margarine. Press about 2/3 of the mixture over the bottom of an 8-inch baking pan. Spread the rhubarb in the prepared pan. Cook the sugar, cornstarch and water in a saucepan over medium heat until thickened, stirring constantly. Add the vanilla and food coloring and pour over the rhubarb. Top with the remaining oats mixture. Bake at 350 degrees for 45 minutes. Serve warm or cold.

YIELD: 9 SERVINGS

A mother's heart is the child's schoolroom.

—*Henry Ward Beecher*

Russian Berry Cream

2 pints fresh blackberries or raspberries
1/2 cup sugar
1/2 cup water
1 (3-ounce) package cranberry or
   raspberry gelatin

Ginger ale
Whipped cream or whipped topping
Slivered almonds

Rinse the berries and drain. Combine the berries with the sugar and water in a saucepan. Bring to a boil, reduce the heat and simmer for about 15 minutes or until the berries are very soft. Press the berry mixture through a colander into a small bowl. Strain the sieved berries, pressing to extract the maximum amount of juice and discard the seeds.

Dissolve the gelatin according to the package directions, substituting ginger ale for all or any portion of the water. Stir the berry juice into the dissolved gelatin. Pour the mixture into a 1 1/2-quart mold or casserole and chill until firm.

Unmold the gelatin onto a serving plate. Spread the gelatin with whipped cream and sprinkle with slivered almonds. Spoon into glass dessert dishes or parfait glasses.

YIELD: 6 TO 8 SERVINGS

Éclair Ring

2 (4-ounce) packages vanilla instant
   pudding mix
2 1/2 cups milk
2 cups whipping cream
1 teaspoon vanilla extract
1 cup water

1/2 cup (1 stick) butter
1 cup flour
1 teaspoon salt
4 eggs
1 recipe favorite chocolate frosting

Prepare the pudding mix with the milk according to the package directions. Beat the whipping cream in a mixing bowl until soft peaks form, adding the vanilla gradually. Fold the whipped cream into the pudding mixture. Chill, covered, in the refrigerator.

Combine the water and butter in a large saucepan. Bring to a boil and remove from the heat. Add the flour and salt all at once and mix vigorously until the mixture pulls from the side of the pan and forms a ball. Add the eggs 1 at a time and beat vigorously until well blended after each addition. Drop the batter by spoonfuls onto a greased baking sheet to form a ring. Bake at 400 degrees for 40 minutes. Turn off the oven and leave the baking sheet in the oven for 15 minutes longer. Remove the baking sheet to a wire rack to cool.

Cut the ring crosswise into 2 layers and scoop out any uncooked dough. Spoon the pudding mixture into the cavities, replace the top and frost with chocolate frosting.

YIELD: 6 SERVINGS

CREAM PUFF DESSERT

1 cup water
1/2 cup (1 stick) margarine
1 cup flour
4 eggs
1 (6-ounce) package vanilla instant
   pudding mix

3 cups milk
8 ounces cream cheese, softened
8 ounces whipped topping
Chocolate syrup

Combine the water and margarine in a medium saucepan. Bring to a boil and add the flour all at once, mixing vigorously until the mixture forms a ball. Remove from the heat. Add the eggs 1 at a time, beating vigorously after each addition until completely blended. Spread over the bottom of a lightly greased 9×13-inch baking pan. Bake at 400 degrees for 30 minutes. Let stand until completely cooled.

Prepare the pudding mix with the milk in a large mixing bowl according to the package directions. Add the cream cheese and beat until blended. Spread the mixture over the baked crust. Spread the whipped topping over the pudding layer and drizzle chocolate syrup over the top. Chill until serving time.

YIELD: 12 TO 15 SERVINGS

EASY ÉCLAIR DESSERT

Graham crackers
2 (4-ounce) packages French vanilla
   instant pudding mix

3 cups milk
8 to 9 ounces whipped topping
1 (16-ounce) can chocolate fudge frosting

Line a 9×13-inch dish sprayed with nonstick cooking spray with graham crackers. Prepare the pudding mix with the milk according to the package directions. Fold in the whipped topping. Cover the graham crackers with half the pudding mixture. Add layers of additional graham crackers, the remaining pudding mixture and a final layer of graham crackers. Open the frosting and microwave for 1 minute or until softened to a pourable consistency. Spread the frosting over the graham crackers. Chill for 1 hour or longer.

YIELD: 12 SERVINGS

Luscious Layered Chocolate Squares

1 cup self-rising flour
1/2 cup (1 stick) margarine
1 cup chopped pecans
8 ounces cream cheese, softened
3/4 cup sugar
1 cup whipped topping
1 1/2 cups sugar
3 tablespoons cornstarch

3 tablespoons baking cocoa
3 egg yolks, beaten
1 cup milk
3 tablespoons margarine
2 teaspoons vanilla extract
Whipped topping
Grated chocolate

Combine the flour and 1/2 cup margarine in a bowl and cut together until crumbly. Add the pecans and mix well. Press the mixture evenly over the bottom of a 9×13-inch baking dish. Bake at 350 degrees for 15 minutes or until golden brown. Let stand until cool.

Beat the cream cheese, 3/4 cup sugar and 1 cup whipped topping in a mixing bowl until smooth and creamy. Spread the mixture evenly over the cooled crust.

Combine 1 1/2 cups sugar, cornstarch and baking cocoa in a saucepan and mix well. Beat the egg yolks with the milk and add to the baking cocoa mixture, blending well. Cook the mixture over low heat until smooth and thickened, stirring constantly. Remove from the heat and stir in 3 tablespoons margarine and vanilla. Let stand until cool.

Spread the cooled mixture over the cream cheese layer. Spread the desired amount of whipped topping over the top and sprinkle with desired amount of grated chocolate. Refrigerate until serving time. Cut into 3-inch squares.

YIELD: 8 SERVINGS

For his heart was in his work, and the heart
giveth grace unto every art.

—*Henry Wadsworth Longfellow*

MOCHA CHIP ICE CREAM

2 cups heavy cream
2 cups milk
1/4 cup instant coffee granules
4 eggs
13/4 cups sugar
1/2 (14-ounce) can sweetened
    condensed milk

1/4 teaspoon salt
1 (1-ounce) square unsweetened baking
    chocolate, grated
2 cups heavy cream
1 teaspoon vanilla extract
1 (1-ounce) square semisweet chocolate,
    grated

Combine 2 cups heavy cream and milk in a saucepan and heat but do not boil. Remove from the heat and add the coffee granules and stir until completely dissolved. Beat the eggs with the sugar, condensed milk and salt in a medium mixing bowl. Stir a small amount of the hot mixture into the egg mixture and stir the egg mixture into the hot mixture.

Return the saucepan to medium heat. Add the unsweetened chocolate and cook to 176 degrees on a candy thermometer, stirring constantly. Remove from the heat and refrigerate until thoroughly chilled.

Pour the mixture into an ice cream freezer container. Add 2 cups heavy cream, vanilla and semisweet chocolate. Freeze according to the manufacturer's instructions.

YIELD: 1 GALLON

The feeling of friendship is like that of being comfortably filled with
roast beef; love, like being enlivened with champagne.

—*Samuel Johnson*

Date Pudding with Brown Sugar Sauce

8 ounces pitted dates, chopped
1 cup boiling water
1 cup sugar
1/2 (1 stick) butter, softened
1 egg
2 cups flour

1 teaspoon baking soda
1/2 teaspoon baking powder
1/8 teaspoon salt
1 teaspoon vanilla extract
1/2 cup chopped nuts
Brown Sugar Sauce

Place the dates in a small bowl. Add the boiling water and let stand until cool. Cream the sugar and butter in a mixing bowl until light and fluffy. Add the egg and mix well. Combine the flour, baking soda, baking powder and salt in a bowl and mix well. Add to the creamed mixture alternately with the date mixture, mixing well after each addition. Add the vanilla and the nuts and mix well. Pour the batter into a greased loaf pan.

Bake at 350 degrees for 1 hour. Let the pudding stand for several minutes then invert onto a serving plate. Slice the pudding and serve the Brown Sugar Sauce hot or cold over the pudding slices.

YIELD: 8 TO 10 SERVINGS

Brown Sugar Sauce

1 tablespoon butter
1 tablespoon flour
1 cup packed brown sugar

1 cup boiling water
1 egg, well beaten
1 teaspoon vanilla extract

Melt the butter in a saucepan. Add the flour and brown sugar and blend well. Stir in the boiling water and cook until thickened, stirring constantly. Stir a small amount of the hot mixture into the beaten egg; stir the egg into the hot mixture and mix well. Remove from the heat and blend in the vanilla.

INDIAN PUDDING

This is a traditional late 1800s recipe from Maine. It was usually made on Saturdays when beans were being baked in a slow oven for hours.

2 cups milk
3 tablespoons (heaping) cornmeal
1 tablespoon butter or margarine

1 cup molasses (not blackstrap)
1/2 teaspoon salt
4 cups milk

Bring 2 cups milk to a gentle simmer in a large heavy ovenproof saucepan. Sprinkle the cornmeal over the top gradually, stirring constantly until the mixture is thickened; do not allow to boil. Add the butter, molasses and salt and mix well. Stir in 2 cups of the remaining milk. Place the pan in the oven.

Bake at 300 degrees for 1 hour, stirring occasionally. Stir in 1 cup of the remaining milk. Bake for 1 hour, stirring occasionally. Stir in the remaining 1 cup milk. Bake until the pudding is thickened to the desired consistency; it is best if nearly caramelized. Serve the pudding warm with the best quality vanilla ice cream.

YIELD: 4 SERVINGS

LEMON CAKE AND CUSTARD PUDDING

This is a comforting but not too sweet dessert.

3 tablespoons butter or margarine,
   softened
1 cup sugar
4 egg yolks
3 tablespoons flour

1/4 cup lemon juice
2 teaspoons grated lemon peel
1 cup milk
4 egg whites, stiffly beaten

Cream the butter and sugar in a mixing bowl until light and fluffy. Add the egg yolks and beat until blended. Add the flour, lemon juice and peel and beat until smooth. Beat in the milk gradually. Fold in the stiffly beaten egg whites gently. Divide the batter among 8 greased custard cups.

Arrange the custard cups in a 10×15-inch baking dish and add hot water to the baking dish to a depth of 1 inch. Bake at 350 degrees for 40 minutes. Place the custard cups on serving plates. The custard will be on the bottom and the cake on the top.

YIELD: 8 SERVINGS

Lemon Pudding Pie Dessert

1¹/₂ cups flour
³/₄ cup (1¹/₂ sticks) butter or margarine
8 ounces cream cheese, softened
1 cup confectioners' sugar

8 ounces whipped topping
2 (4-ounce) packages lemon pudding and
    pie filling mix
Whipped topping

Place the flour in a bowl. Cut in the butter until the mixture is crumbly. Press the mixture into a greased 9×13-inch baking pan. Bake at 375 degrees for 15 minutes. Let stand until cool. Beat the cream cheese with the confectioners' sugar in a mixing bowl until smooth and creamy. Fold in 8 ounces whipped topping. Spread the mixture over the cooled crust. Prepare the pudding mix according to the package directions. Spread over the cream cheese layer. Top with additional whipped topping. Refrigerate until serving time.

YIELD: 12 SERVINGS

Lemon Torte with Raspberries

1 small package sugar-free lemon gelatin
¹/₂ cup boiling water
¹/₂ cup frozen lemonade concentrate,
    thawed

1 (12-ounce) can evaporated skim milk
2 cups angel food cake cubes
2 cups fresh raspberries
1 tablespoon sugar

Combine the gelatin and the boiling water in a mixing bowl, stirring until the gelatin is completely dissolved. Add the lemonade concentrate and evaporated milk and mix well. Chill, covered, for 1¹/₂ hours or until the mixture mounds when dropped from a spoon. Beat the mixture with an electric mixer at medium to high speed for 8 to 10 minutes or until fluffy.

Arrange the cake cubes in an 8-inch springform pan sprayed with nonstick cooking spray. Pour the lemon mixture over the cake. Refrigerate for 4 hours or until firm. Mix the raspberries with the sugar and chill for 2 hours. Loosen the torte from the side of the pan and remove the side of the pan. Cut into wedges and top with the sweetened raspberries.

YIELD: 10 SERVINGS

The wise man looks inside his heart and finds eternal peace.
—*Hindu Proverb*

Punch Bowl Cake

1 (2-layer) package yellow cake mix
1 (6-ounce) package vanilla instant
    pudding mix
3 cups milk
6 bananas, sliced

1 (20-ounce) can crushed pineapple,
    drained
2 (21-ounce) cans strawberry pie filling
16 ounces whipped topping
2 cups crushed pecans

Prepare and bake the cake according to the package directions and cool completely. Prepare the pudding mix with the milk according to the package directions. Tear the cake into small pieces.

Place $^1/_2$ the cake pieces in a large punch bowl and add layers of $^1/_2$ the banana slices, $^1/_2$ the prepared pudding and $^1/_2$ the pineapple. Add 1 can of pie filling, $^1/_2$ the whipped topping and 1 cup of the pecans. Repeat the layers. Garnish with sliced fresh strawberries if desired. Refrigerate, covered, until serving time. Scoop through all the layers when serving.

YIELD: 12 TO 15 SERVINGS

Strawberry Delight

$2^1/_2$ cups graham cracker crumbs
$^1/_2$ cup sugar
$^2/_3$ cup margarine, melted
2 (3-ounce) packages strawberry gelatin
2 cups boiling water
2 (10-ounce) packages frozen strawberries

12 ounces cream cheese, softened
9 ounces whipped topping
2 cups confectioners' sugar
$^1/_2$ cup chopped nuts
Whipped topping

Combine the graham cracker crumbs, sugar and melted margarine in a bowl and mix well. Press the mixture evenly over the bottom of a 9×13-inch dish. Dissolve the gelatin in the boiling water in a large bowl. Add the frozen strawberries and stir until the strawberries thaw. Chill until partially set.

Combine the cream cheese, 9 ounces whipped topping and confectioners' sugar in a mixing bowl and mix until well blended. Stir in the nuts. Spread the mixture over the crumb layer. Spoon the partially congealed strawberry mixture over the cream cheese layer. Chill until set. Top with additional whipped topping if desired. Cut into squares.

YIELD: 12 TO 15 SERVINGS

APPLE CAKE

4 Winesap or McIntosh apples
2/3 cup sugar
1 teaspoon cinnamon
2 cups sugar
1/4 cup orange juice
1 cup vegetable oil

2 1/2 teaspoons vanilla extract
4 eggs, beaten
3 cups flour
1 tablespoon baking powder
1/8 teaspoon salt

Peel, core and slice the apples and set aside. Mix 2/3 cup sugar with the cinnamon in a small bowl and set aside. Combine 2 cups sugar, orange juice, oil, vanilla and eggs in a mixing bowl and stir until well mixed. Mix the flour, baking powder and salt together. Add to the egg mixture and mix well. Pour 1/2 the batter into a greased tube or bundt pan. Add a layer of 1/2 the apples and sprinkle with 1/2 the cinnamon-sugar. Repeat the layers. Bake at 350 degrees for 1 1/4 to 1 1/2 hours or until the cake tests done. Cool in the pan on a wire rack for 10 minutes. Invert the cake onto a serving plate.

YIELD: 12 TO 16 SERVINGS

APPLESAUCE FRUITCAKE

1 1/2 cups sweetened applesauce
1/2 cup shortening
1 cup sugar
1 (8-ounce) package pitted dates, sliced
2 cups chopped walnuts or pecans
1 (4-ounce) jar red glacé cherries,
    chopped or mixed candied fruit

2 cups seedless raisins
2 1/4 cups sifted flour
2 teaspoons baking soda
1/2 teaspoon salt
1 teaspoon cinnamon
1/2 teaspoon nutmeg
1/2 teaspoon allspice

Grease a 9-inch tube pan, line with foil, grease the foil and set aside. Combine the applesauce, shortening and sugar in a saucepan. Bring to a boil and cook for 5 minutes, stirring frequently. Let stand until cool. Combine the dates, walnuts, cherries and raisins in a large bowl and toss to mix. Sift the flour, baking soda, salt and spices together. Add the flour mixture to the fruit mixture gradually, mixing well after each addition. Add the applesauce mixture and mix well. Pour the batter into the prepared tube pan.

Bake at 275 degrees for 2 hours or until a cake tester inserted in the center comes out clean. Cool the cake in the pan on a wire rack for 30 minutes. Invert the cake onto a serving plate and remove the foil. Let stand until completely cool before slicing. Store the cake tightly wrapped in an airtight container.

YIELD: 16 SERVINGS

BLACK BOTTOM CUPCAKES

8 ounces cream cheese, softened
$^1/_3$ cup confectioners' sugar
$^1/_8$ teaspoon salt
1 cup chocolate chips
$^1/_3$ cup chopped nuts (optional)
$^1/_4$ cup sugar
1$^1/_2$ cups flour
$^1/_2$ teaspoon salt

1 teaspoon baking soda
1 cup sugar
$^1/_4$ cup baking cocoa
1 cup water
$^1/_3$ cup vegetable oil
1 tablespoon vinegar
1 teaspoon vanilla extract

Combine the cream cheese, confectioners' sugar and $^1/_8$ teaspoon salt in a mixing bowl and beat until smooth and creamy. Stir in $^3/_4$ cup of the chocolate chips and set aside. Combine the remaining $^1/_4$ cup chocolate chips, the nuts and $^1/_4$ cup sugar in a small bowl, mix well and set aside. Sift the flour, $^1/_2$ teaspoon salt, baking soda, 1 cup sugar and baking cocoa into a mixing bowl. Add the water, oil, vinegar and vanilla and beat until well blended.

Divide the batter among 18 greased muffin cups or paper-lined muffin cups. Add a spoonful of the cream cheese mixture to each and top with the nut mixture. Bake at 350 degrees for 25 to 30 minutes or until a wooden pick inserted in the centers comes out clean.

YIELD: 18 SERVINGS

HOT FUDGE CAKE

1 cup flour
$^3/_4$ cup sugar
2 tablespoons baking cocoa
2 teaspoons baking powder
$^1/_4$ teaspoon salt
$^1/_2$ cup milk

2 tablespoons vegetable oil
1 teaspoon vanilla extract
1 cup packed brown sugar
$^1/_4$ cup baking cocoa
1$^3/_4$ cups hot water

Combine the flour, sugar, 2 tablespoons baking cocoa, baking powder and salt in a mixing bowl and mix well. Add the milk, oil and vanilla and mix well. Pour the mixture into an ungreased 9-inch square baking pan. Mix the brown sugar and $^1/_4$ cup baking cocoa in a small bowl and sprinkle over the batter.

Pour the hot water over the top and do not stir. Bake at 350 degrees for 35 to 40 minutes or until the cake tests done. The cake will be on the top and the chocolate sauce will be on the bottom. Serve a warm portion of the cake with the chocolate sauce spooned over the top and add a dollop of whipped cream or ice cream.

YIELD: 6 TO 8 SERVINGS

Oatmeal Chocolate Chip Cake

1 cup rolled oats
$^1/_2$ cup (1 stick) margarine
$1^3/_4$ cups boiling water
1 cup sugar
1 cup packed brown sugar
2 eggs

$1^3/_4$ cups flour
1 teaspoon baking soda
$^1/_2$ teaspoon salt
1 teaspoon baking cocoa
2 cups chocolate chips
$^3/_4$ cup chopped nuts

Combine the oats and margarine in a large mixing bowl. Pour the boiling water over the top and let stand for 10 minutes. Add the sugars and mix well. Add the eggs and mix well. Sift the flour, baking soda, salt and baking cocoa together. Add to the oats mixture and mix well. Stir in 1 cup of the chocolate chips. Pour into a greased and floured 9×13-inch cake pan. Sprinkle the remaining chocolate chips and nuts over the top. Bake at 350 degrees for 30 minutes or until the cake tests done.

YIELD: 12 TO 15 SERVINGS

Cranberry Orange Torte

$2^1/_4$ cups sifted flour
1 cup sugar
1 teaspoon baking powder
1 teaspoon baking soda
$^1/_4$ teaspoon salt
1 cup chopped walnuts
1 cup fresh whole cranberries
1 cup chopped dates

Grated peel of 2 oranges
2 eggs
$^1/_2$ cup sour cream
$^1/_2$ cup milk
$^3/_4$ cup vegetable oil
1 cup orange juice
1 cup sugar

Sift the flour, 1 cup sugar, baking powder, baking soda and salt into a large bowl. Add the walnuts, cranberries, dates and orange peel and mix well. Beat the eggs in a medium bowl. Blend the sour cream and milk together and add to the eggs. Blend in the oil and add to the cranberry mixture, mixing well. Pour the batter into a greased and floured 10-inch tube pan.

Bake at 350 degrees for 1 hour or until the cake tests done. Cool in the pan on a wire rack for 10 minutes. Mix the orange juice with the 1 cup sugar in a bowl until the sugar dissolves. Pour the mixture over the warm cake in the pan. Let stand for 30 minutes. Invert the cake onto a large piece of heavy duty foil. Wrap the cake tightly in the foil and refrigerate for 24 hours to 2 weeks.

YIELD: 10 TO 12 SERVINGS

CINNAMON CHIFFON TORTE

1 cup sifted cake flour
1 teaspoon baking powder
1 teaspoon cinnamon
8 egg whites
1/8 teaspoon salt

1/2 cup sugar
8 egg yolks
1/2 cup sugar
1 teaspoon vanilla extract
Chocolate Whipped Cream Frosting

Sift the cake flour, baking powder and cinnamon together 3 times and set aside. Beat the egg whites and salt in a large mixing bowl with an electric mixer at high speed until soft peaks form. Add 1/2 cup sugar gradually, beating constantly. Beat until stiff but not dry peaks form and set aside. Beat the egg yolks in a medium mixing bowl until thick and lemon-colored. Add 1/2 cup sugar gradually, beating until thick and pale yellow. Beat in the vanilla. Fold the egg yolk mixture into the stiffly beaten egg whites gently. Fold in the sifted dry ingredients gently. Pour the batter into an ungreased 10-inch tube pan.

Bake at 350 degrees for 40 to 45 minutes or until golden brown and the cake springs back when touched lightly. Invert the cake pan on a funnel to cool. Loosen the cake from the side of the pan. Invert the cake onto a wire rack.

Split the cake into 3 layers. Spread the Chocolate Whipped Cream Frosting between the layers and over the top and side of the cake.

YIELD: 12 SERVINGS

CHOCOLATE WHIPPED CREAM FROSTING

3 cups whipping cream
3/4 cup sugar

1/3 cup baking cocoa
1 teaspoon vanilla extract

Combine the whipping cream, sugar, baking cocoa and vanilla in a mixing bowl and mix well. Refrigerate for 4 hours or longer. Beat with an electric mixer at high speed until stiff peaks form.

The most evident sign of wisdom is continued cheerfulness.
—*Michel de Montaigne*

CINNAMON CAKE SQUARES

This small, quick cake requires no frosting and is also delicious as a coffee cake.

1¹/₂ cups flour
2 teaspoons baking powder
¹/₂ teaspoon salt
1 teaspoon cinnamon
1 cup sugar
2 eggs

¹/₃ cup shortening
¹/₂ cup milk
1 teaspoon vanilla extract
2 tablespoons confectioners' sugar
¹/₂ teaspoon cinnamon

Sift the flour, baking powder, salt and 1 teaspoon cinnamon into a large mixing bowl. Add the sugar and mix well. Add the eggs, shortening, milk and vanilla and beat with an electric mixer at medium speed for 2 minutes, scraping the bowl occasionally. Pour the batter into a greased and floured 8- or 9-inch square cake pan. Mix the confectioners' sugar and ¹/₂ teaspoon cinnamon together and sprinkle over the batter. Bake at 375 degrees for 20 to 25 minutes or until the cake tests done.

YIELD: 6 TO 8 SERVINGS

DATE NUT RING

*Serve the cake plain as a coffee cake for breakfast or brunch, or
with whipped topping as a dessert.*

2 cups pitted date halves
3 cups chopped nuts
1 cup sifted flour
¹/₂ teaspoon salt

1 cup sugar
4 egg whites
4 egg yolks
1 teaspoon vanilla extract

Combine the dates and nuts in a large bowl. Add the flour, salt and sugar and mix well. Beat the egg whites in a mixing bowl until stiff peaks form and set aside. Beat the egg yolks with the vanilla in a small bowl until the mixture is thick and pale yellow. Add the egg yolk mixture to the date mixture and mix well. Fold the stiffly beaten egg whites into the date mixture. Spoon the batter into a greased 10-inch tube pan. Bake at 350 degrees for 50 to 60 minutes or until a wooden pick inserted in the center comes out clean. Cool and invert onto a cake plate.

YIELD: 12 SERVINGS

HUMMINGBIRD CAKE

Enjoy this moist cake with or without the nuts or even without the frosting.

3 cups flour
2 cups sugar
1 teaspoon salt
1 teaspoon baking soda
1 teaspoon cinnamon
3 eggs, beaten
1¹/₂ cups vegetable oil

1 (8-ounce) can crushed pineapple
1 cup chopped pecans or walnuts
2 cups chopped very ripe bananas
1¹/₂ teaspoons vanilla extract
Cream Cheese Frosting
1 cup chopped pecans or walnuts

Mix the flour, sugar, salt, baking soda and cinnamon in a large bowl. Add the eggs and oil and stir just until the dry ingredients are moistened. Add the undrained pineapple, 1 cup pecans, bananas and vanilla and mix well.

Spoon the batter into 3 greased and floured 9-inch cake pans. Bake at 350 degrees for 25 minutes or until the layers test done. Cool in the pans on wire racks for 10 minutes. Remove the layers to wire racks to cool completely.

Spread the Cream Cheese Frosting between the layers and over the top and side of the cake. Sprinkle 1 cup pecans over the top.

YIELD: 16 SERVINGS

CREAM CHEESE FROSTING

8 ounces cream cheese, softened
¹/₂ cup (1 stick) butter or margarine,
   softened

1 (1-pound) package confectioners' sugar
2 teaspoons vanilla extract

Combine the cream cheese and butter in a mixing bowl and beat until smooth and well blended. Add the confectioners' sugar gradually, beating until light and fluffy. Add the vanilla and beat until well blended.

You can do anything if you have enthusiasm. It is the yeast
that makes your hopes rise to the stars.

—Henry Ford

ORANGE SPONGE CAKE

Light as a feather and not too sweet. Use a serrated knife for easier cutting.

8 egg whites, at room temperature
1/4 teaspoon salt
1 teaspoon cream of tartar
2/3 cup sugar
8 egg yolks, at room temperature

2/3 cup sugar
1/4 cup orange juice
Grated peel of 1 orange
1 cup plus 2 tablespoons flour
Orange Topping

Beat the egg whites with the salt in a large mixing bowl with an electric mixer at high speed until foamy. Add the cream of tartar and beat until well mixed. Add 2/3 cup sugar gradually, beating constantly until stiff glossy peaks form and set aside. Beat the egg yolks in a small mixing bowl until well blended. Add 2/3 cup sugar, orange juice and orange peel and beat until thick and pale yellow. Add the egg yolk mixture to the egg whites, beating at low speed just until blended. Add the flour and beat at low speed just until blended, scraping the bowl frequently.

Spoon the batter into an ungreased 10-inch tube pan. Cut through the batter with a table knife to release the bubbles. Bake at 325 degrees for 60 to 70 minutes or until brown and a wooden pick inserted in the center comes out clean.

Invert the pan on a wire rack to cool completely. Loosen the cake from the side of the pan with a thin sharp knife and invert onto a cake plate. Pour the Orange Topping over the cake.

YIELD: 16 SERVINGS

ORANGE TOPPING

6 tablespoons frozen orange juice
   concentrate, thawed
6 tablespoons water

1/2 cup sugar
1 tablespoon cornstarch

Combine the orange juice concentrate, water, sugar and cornstarch in a small saucepan and mix well. Cook over medium heat until clear and thickened, stirring constantly. Cool slightly.

Coconut Walnut Pound Cake

2 cups sugar
4 eggs, beaten
1 cup vegetable oil
3 cups flour
1/2 teaspoon baking soda
1/2 teaspoon baking powder

1/2 teaspoon salt
1 cup buttermilk
2 teaspoons coconut extract
1 cup chopped walnuts
1 cup flaked coconut
Coconut Syrup

Combine the sugar, eggs and oil in a mixing bowl and beat until well blended. Mix the flour, baking soda, baking powder and salt in a bowl. Add the dry ingredients to the sugar mixture alternately with the buttermilk, beating well after each addition. Beat in the coconut flavoring. Add the walnuts and coconut and stir until well mixed.

Pour the batter into a greased and floured tube pan. Bake at 325 degrees for 60 to 65 minutes or until the cake tests done. Poke many holes in the cake with a wooden pick.

Pour the hot Coconut Syrup over the hot cake slowly to allow the syrup to soak into the cake. Let the cake cool in the pan for 30 minutes to 1 hour before inverting onto a cake plate.

YIELD: 12 TO 16 SERVINGS

Coconut Syrup

1 cup sugar
2 tablespoons margarine

1/2 cup water
1 teaspoon coconut extract

Combine the sugar, margarine and water in a small saucepan. Bring to a boil, stirring until the sugar dissolves. Boil for 5 minutes. Remove from the heat and stir in the coconut flavoring.

It is not by the gray of the hair that one knows the age of the heart.

—*Bulwer*

CREAM CHEESE POUND CAKE

1¹/₂ cups (3 sticks) butter
8 ounces cream cheese
2¹/₃ cups sugar

6 eggs
3 cups flour
1 teaspoon vanilla extract

Let all the ingredients come to room temperature. Combine the butter and cream cheese in a large mixing bowl and beat until smooth and well blended. Add the sugar gradually, beating constantly. Beat for 5 to 7 minutes or until light and fluffy. Add the eggs 1 at a time, beating well after each addition. Add the flour gradually, beating just until blended after each addition. Beat in the vanilla. Pour the batter into a greased and floured 10-inch tube pan. Bake at 300 degrees for 1¹/₂ hours or until the cake tests done. Cool in the pan on a wire rack for 15 minutes. Invert the cake onto a wire rack to cool completely.

YIELD: 12 TO 16 SERVINGS

PURPLE PLUM TORTE

Prune plums have a very limited season, so plan ahead. Buy the plums, cut into halves, and discard the pits. Spread in a single layer on a tray or baking sheet to freeze and then store in bags in recipe-size portions. It is not necessary to thaw the plums before using.

¹/₂ cup (1 stick) butter, softened
1 cup sugar
2 eggs
1 cup sifted flour

1 teaspoon baking powder
¹/₈ teaspoon salt
12 Italian prune plums
Sugar, lemon juice and cinnamon to taste

Cream the butter and sugar in a mixing bowl until light and fluffy. Beat in the eggs. Mix the flour, baking powder and salt together, add to the creamed mixture and beat until well blended. Pour the batter into a greased 9-inch springform pan.

Cut the plums lengthwise into halves and discard the pits. Arrange the plums cut side down on the batter to cover the entire surface. Sprinkle with sugar, lemon juice and a generous amount of cinnamon. Bake at 350 degrees for 1 hour. Cool slightly. Loosen from the side of the pan and remove the side of the pan. Serve slightly warm with vanilla ice cream.

YIELD: 6 TO 8 SERVINGS

TROPICAL DELIGHT CAKE

1 (2-layer) package lemon cake mix
1 cup vegetable oil
4 eggs
1 (8-ounce) can mandarin oranges

Pineapple Lemon Frosting
1 (8-ounce) can mandarin oranges,
  well drained

Combine the cake mix, oil, eggs and undrained mandarin oranges in a large mixing bowl and beat until well mixed. Pour the batter into a greased and floured tube pan. Bake at 350 degrees for 35 to 45 minutes or until the cake tests done. Cool the cake in the pan for 10 to 15 minutes. Invert onto a cake plate to cool completely.

Split the cake into 2 layers. Spread the Pineapple Lemon Frosting between the layers and over the top and side of the cake. Decorate the cake with the well drained mandarin oranges. Store the cake in the refrigerator.

YIELD: 10 TO 12 SERVINGS

PINEAPPLE LEMON FROSTING

16 ounces whipped topping
1 (4-ounce) package lemon instant
  pudding mix

1 (20-ounce) can crushed pineapple,
  drained

Place the whipped topping in a mixing bowl. Sprinkle the pudding mix over the whipped topping. Add the crushed pineapple and stir until well mixed.

There is in friendship something of all relations, and something above them all.
It is the golden thread that ties the heart of all the world.

—John Evelyn

Pumpkin Cake Roll

3 eggs
1 cup sugar
2/3 cup pumpkin
1 teaspoon lemon juice
3/4 cup flour
1 teaspoon baking powder
1/2 teaspoon salt

2 teaspoons cinnamon
1 teaspoon ginger
1/2 teaspoon nutmeg
1 cup finely chopped walnuts
Confectioners' sugar
Cream Cheese Filling

Beat the eggs in a mixing bowl with an electric mixer at high speed for 5 minutes. Add the sugar gradually, beating constantly until blended. Add the pumpkin and lemon juice and mix well. Mix the flour, baking powder, salt, cinnamon, ginger and nutmeg together. Fold the flour mixture into the pumpkin mixture.

Spread the batter in a greased and floured 10×15-inch jelly roll pan. Sprinkle the walnuts over the top. Bake at 375 degrees for 15 minutes.

Invert the hot cake onto a towel generously dusted with confectioners' sugar. Roll the cake in the towel as for a jelly roll and let stand until cool. Unroll the cake carefully. Spread the cake with the Cream Cheese Filling and reroll. Place the cake seam side down on a serving plate. Chill until serving time. Garnish with whipped cream.

YIELD: 8 SERVINGS

Cream Cheese Filling

4 to 6 ounces cream cheese, softened
1/4 cup (1/2 stick) butter, softened

1 cup confectioners' sugar
1/2 teaspoon vanilla extract

Combine the cream cheese and butter in a mixing bowl and beat until well blended. Add the confectioners' sugar and beat until smooth and creamy. Beat in the vanilla.

Where we love is home. Home that our
feet may leave but not our hearts.

—*Oliver Wendell Holmes, Jr.*

RHUBARB CAKE

2 cups flour
1 teaspoon baking soda
1/4 teaspoon salt
1 1/2 cups packed brown sugar
1/2 cup (1 stick) margarine, softened
1 egg

1 cup milk
1 teaspoon vanilla extract
2 1/2 cups chopped rhubarb
1/2 cup sugar
1 teaspoon cinnamon

Mix the flour, baking soda and salt in a bowl and set aside. Cream the brown sugar and margarine in a mixing bowl until light and fluffy. Add the egg and beat until well blended. Add the flour mixture alternately with the milk, beating well after each addition. Beat in the vanilla. Add the rhubarb and stir until well mixed.

Pour the batter into a greased and floured 9×13-inch cake pan. Mix the sugar and cinnamon together and sprinkle over the batter. Bake at 350 degrees for 40 minutes or until a wooden pick inserted in the center comes out clean. Store the cake in the refrigerator after cutting.

YIELD: 12 TO 15 SERVINGS

STRAWBERRY RHUBARB CAKE

4 cups (1/2-inch pieces) rhubarb
1 cup sugar
3/4 cup water
2 cups flour
2 teaspoons baking powder
1/2 teaspoon salt
2/3 cup shortening or margarine

1 1/4 cups sugar
2 eggs
1 teaspoon vanilla extract
1 1/3 cups milk
1 1/4 cups sliced fresh strawberries
Cinnamon to taste

Combine the rhubarb, 1 cup sugar and water in a saucepan. Bring to a simmer, stirring until the sugar dissolves. Simmer for 10 minutes, stirring occasionally. Set the rhubarb aside but keep warm. Sift the flour, baking powder and salt together and set aside. Cream the shortening and 1 1/4 cups sugar in a mixing bowl until light and fluffy. Add the eggs and vanilla and beat until smooth. Add the sifted dry ingredients alternately with the milk, beating well after each addition.

Pour the batter into a greased 9×13-inch cake pan. Layer the sliced strawberries over the batter. Spoon the rhubarb mixture over the strawberries and sprinkle with cinnamon. Bake at 350 degrees for 35 minutes. Serve with whipped cream or ice cream.

YIELD: 10 TO 12 SERVINGS

APPLE PIE IN A BAG

6 large McIntosh apples
1/2 cup sugar
2 tablespoons flour
2 teaspoons cinnamon
1 1/2 cups flour
1 teaspoon salt

2 teaspoons sugar
1/2 cup vegetable oil
1 tablespoon milk
1/2 cup sugar
1/2 cup flour
1/3 cup butter or margarine, melted

Peel, core and slice the apples and place in a large bowl. Add 1/2 cup sugar, 2 tablespoons flour and cinnamon and mix well. Combine 1 1/2 cups flour, salt and 2 teaspoons sugar in a small bowl. Add the oil and milk and mix well. Press the mixture over the bottom and up the side of a 9-inch pie plate to form a crust. Mound the apple slices in the crust. Combine 1/2 cup sugar, 1/2 cup flour and melted butter in a bowl and mix well. Spread the mixture evenly over the apples. Place the pie in a large clean brown paper bag. (Editor's note: Be sure that the bag is not made of recycled material.) Fold the ends together several times and staple to secure. Cut several 1/2-inch slits in the bag to allow the steam to escape. Place the oven rack on the second level from the bottom and place the bag directly on the rack but do not allow the bag to touch the oven sides or top. Bake at 425 degrees for 1 hour. Let the pie cool in the bag for 5 to 10 minutes, then cut the bag from around the pie with scissors.

YIELD: 8 SERVINGS

SOUR CREAM APPLE PIE

2 cups chopped peeled apples
3/4 cup sugar
2 tablespoons flour
1/8 teaspoon salt
1 egg, beaten
1/4 cup sour cream
1 teaspoon vanilla extract

1 unbaked (8-inch) pie shell
1/4 cup flour
3 tablespoons sugar
1/2 teaspoon cinnamon
1/8 teaspoon salt
2 tablespoons butter, softened

Place the apples in a bowl. Add 3/4 cup sugar, 2 tablespoons flour and 1/8 teaspoon salt and toss to coat. Blend the egg, sour cream and vanilla in a small bowl. Add to the the apple mixture and toss to mix. Mound the apple mixture in the pie shell. Bake at 375 degrees for 25 minutes. Combine 1/4 cup flour, 3 tablespoons sugar, cinnamon and 1/8 teaspoon salt in a small bowl and mix well. Add the butter and mix until the mixture is crumbly. Sprinkle over the apple mixture. Bake for 20 minutes longer or until golden brown.

YIELD: 6 TO 8 SERVINGS

CRANBERRY SURPRISE PIE

2 cups cranberries
1/2 cup sugar
1/2 cup chopped walnuts
1 cup sugar

1 cup flour
3/4 cup (1 1/2 sticks) butter, melted
2 eggs, beaten
1 teaspoon almond extract

Rinse the cranberries and drain well. Place the cranberries in a bowl. Add 1/2 cup sugar and walnuts and toss to mix. Place the mixture in a greased 9-inch pie plate. Combine 1 cup sugar, flour, melted butter, eggs and almond flavoring in a bowl and mix well. Spoon the mixture over the cranberries. Bake at 350 degrees for 40 minutes or until golden brown.

YIELD: 6 SERVINGS

CHOCOLATE WALNUT PIE

1/2 cup (1 stick) butter, melted, cooled
3/4 cup sugar
2 eggs, beaten
1 teaspoon vanilla extract

1 cup chopped walnuts
1 cup chocolate chips
1 unbaked pie shell

Combine the melted butter, sugar, eggs and vanilla in a bowl and blend well. Add the walnuts and chocolate chips and stir until well mixed. Pour the mixture into the pie shell. Bake at 375 degrees for 30 minutes or until set. Let stand until cool. Cut into wedges. Serve the wedges with dollops of whipped cream.

YIELD: 8 SERVINGS

To be without some of the things you want is
an indispensable part of happiness.

—Bertrand Russell

German Chocolate Pie

*The Meringue Crust can be filled with a variety of favorite flavors
such as berries or other fruit folded with whipped cream.*

1 (4-ounce) package German's sweet
   chocolate

1 cup whipping cream
Meringue Crust

Break the chocolate into small pieces and melt in a saucepan over low heat or in a microwave-safe dish in the microwave, stirring occasionally. Let stand until cooled. Whip the cream in a mixing bowl until thick. Fold the chocolate and whipped cream together and spread evenly in the Meringue Crust; 1 to 2 inches of the Meringue Crust will still be exposed. Refrigerate for 1 hour or longer.

YIELD: 8 SERVINGS

Meringue Crust

24 butter crackers, crushed
1 cup finely chopped pecans
1/2 cup sugar

3 egg whites
1/2 cup sugar

Combine the cracker crumbs, pecans and 1/2 cup sugar in a bowl and toss to mix. Beat the egg whites in a mixing bowl with an electric mixer at high speed until soft peaks form. Add 1/2 cup sugar gradually, beating constantly until stiff peaks form.

Spread the mixture over the bottom and up the side of a 9-inch deep-dish pie plate. Bake at 325 degrees for 30 minutes. Let stand until completely cool.

*The thread of our life would be dark, Heaven knows!
If it were not with friendship and love intertwin'd.*

—Thomas Moore

PEACHES AND CREAM PIE

³/₄ cup flour
1 teaspoon baking powder
¹/₂ teaspoon salt
1 (4-ounce) package vanilla pudding mix
   (not instant)
3 tablespoons margarine, softened

1 egg, beaten
¹/₂ cup milk
1 (15-ounce) can sliced peaches
8 ounces cream cheese, softened
¹/₂ cup sugar
Cinnamon-sugar to taste

Mix the flour, baking powder, salt and pudding mix in a mixing bowl. Add the margarine, egg and milk and beat until well blended. Spread the mixture over the bottom and up the side of a greased 9-inch pie plate. Drain the peaches, reserving the juice. Arrange the peach slices in a decorative pattern in the prepared pie plate. Combine the cream cheese, sugar and 3 tablespoons of the reserved peach juice in a small mixing bowl and beat for 2 minutes or until smooth. Spoon over the peaches to within 1 inch of the edge. Sprinkle with cinnamon-sugar. Bake at 350 degrees for 30 minutes. Serve warm or cold.

YIELD: 6 SERVINGS

KEY LIME PIE

1 (14-ounce) can sweetened
   condensed milk
4 egg yolks
¹/₂ cup lime juice
1 egg white

1 baked (9-inch) pie shell, cooled
3 egg whites
¹/₂ teaspoon cream of tartar
6 tablespoons sugar

Combine the condensed milk, egg yolks and lime juice in a mixing bowl and whisk until well blended. Beat 1 egg white in a small mixing bowl until stiff peaks form. Fold the stiffly beaten egg white into the lime mixture. Spoon the filling into the cooled pie shell.

Beat 3 egg whites in a mixing bowl with an electric mixer at high speed until soft peaks form. Beat in the cream of tartar. Add the sugar gradually, beating constantly until stiff peaks form. Spread over the top of the pie, sealing to the edge. Bake at 350 degrees for 15 minutes or until golden brown. Let stand until cool. Store in the refrigerator.

YIELD: 8 SERVINGS

Bloom where you are planted.

PECAN PIE

3 eggs

¹/₄ cup packed brown sugar

¹/₂ cup sugar

1 cup light corn syrup

¹/₄ teaspoon salt

1 teaspoon vanilla extract

2 tablespoons butter, melted

1 cup pecan pieces

Pastry Shell

Beat the eggs in a mixing bowl until well blended. Add the brown sugar, sugar, corn syrup, salt, vanilla and melted butter and mix well. Stir in the pecans. Pour the mixture into the Pastry Shell. Bake at 325 degrees for 55 minutes or until a knife inserted in the center comes out clean.

YIELD: 6 SERVINGS

PASTRY SHELL

1¹/₃ cups flour

¹/₂ teaspoon salt

¹/₂ cup butter-flavored shortening

3 tablespoons cold water

Combine the flour and salt in a bowl. Cut in the shortening until crumbly. Add the water gradually, mixing with a fork until the mixture clings together. Shape the mixture into a ball and roll into a circle on a lightly floured surface. Fit the pastry into a 9-inch pie plate, flute the edge and trim the excess pastry.

NEVER-FAIL PIE PASTRY

4 cups flour

2 teaspoons salt

1 tablespoon sugar

1³/₄ cups shortening

¹/₂ cup water

1 egg

1 tablespoon vinegar

Sift the flour, salt and sugar into a bowl. Cut in the shortening until crumbly. Beat the water, egg and vinegar in a small bowl. Add to the flour mixture and mix with a fork until the mixture clings together. Shape into a ball, wrap in plastic wrap and chill for 30 minutes or longer.

Divide the pastry into 6 equal portions. Roll each into a circle and fit into a pie plate, fluting the edge and trimming the excess pastry. Store any unused pastry tightly wrapped in the refrigerator or freezer.

YIELD: 6 PIE SHELLS

Fruit Pizza

8 ounces cream cheese, softened
12 ounces whipped topping
Cookie Crust
Strawberries, blueberries or raspberries
Banana slices

Peach slices
Kiwifruit slices
Grapes
Pineapple chunks
Orange Glaze

Beat the cream cheese and whipped topping in a mixing bowl until smooth and well blended. Spread evenly over desired Cookie Crust. Arrange the fruit decoratively over the top. Spoon the Orange Glaze over the fruit. Refrigerate until serving time. Cut into wedges.

YIELD: 8 TO 12 SERVINGS

Cookie Crust I

1 1/2 cups vanilla wafer crumbs
1/2 cup shredded coconut

1/4 cup chopped nuts
7 tablespoons butter, melted

Combine the crumbs, coconut and nuts in a bowl and toss to mix. Add the butter and mix well. Press over the bottom of a pizza pan and refrigerate for 45 minutes or until firm.

Cookie Crust II

1 (16- to 20-ounce) roll refrigerator
    vanilla or sugar cookie dough

Slice the cookie dough according to the package directions and arrange in a lightly greased pizza pan with the sides of the slices nearly touching. Bake at 350 degrees for 10 minutes or until golden brown. Let cool completely.

Orange Glaze

1/2 cup sugar
2 tablespoons cornstarch
1/2 cup water

1/2 cup orange juice
2 tablespoons lemon juice

Combine the sugar, cornstarch, water, orange juice and lemon juice in a saucepan. Bring to a boil, stirring constantly. Boil until thickened, stirring constantly. Let stand until cool.

COOKIES

Radiant Hearts Quilt
42" × 53"

The Whitney Museum of American Art in New York City put on a show in 1971 entitled *Abstract Design in American Quilts*. Suddenly, quilts, both contemporary and antique, were looked upon as textile art, not merely bed coverings, and began to grace the walls of offices and homes. The women who created the newly prized antique quilts—many whose names will never be known—were seen through new eyes. Their craft had become an art and they were now recognized as the artists they truly were.

A great resurgence in quilting has taken place—starting in the United States and spreading across the globe—since that landmark Whitney Museum exhibition in 1971. Quilting has taken many different forms. Some are firmly based on traditional patterns and techniques; others have used new tools and technology to build on the past, while still others have stretched and changed the definition of quilting in their quest for artistic expression.

PINE NUT ALMOND COOKIES

1 (8-ounce) can almond paste
²/₃ cup sugar
2 egg whites

1 teaspoon grated lemon peel
³/₄ cup pine nuts

Cut the almond paste into small pieces and place in a medium mixing bowl. Add the sugar, egg whites and lemon peel and beat with an electric mixer until smooth. Drop the mixture by teaspoonfuls 1 inch apart onto a cookie sheet lined with parchment paper. Sprinkle with pine nuts and press the nuts lightly into the cookie dough. Bake at 350 degrees for 15 to 20 minutes or until the tops feel firm and dry when touched lightly. Cool the cookies on the cookie sheet on a wire rack. Peel off the parchment and store the cookies in an airtight container at room temperature.

YIELD: 2 DOZEN

APRICOT COCONUT SQUARES

2 cups flour
¹/₄ teaspoon salt
1 cup sugar
³/₄ cup (1¹/₂ sticks) butter or margarine
1 egg

1 teaspoon vanilla extract
1 cup shredded coconut
¹/₂ cup chopped nuts
1 (12-ounce) jar apricot preserves

Combine the flour, salt and sugar in a bowl and mix well. Add the butter and mix with a fork until crumbly. Add the egg and the vanilla, mixing well. Stir in the coconut and nuts. Press about ³/₄ of the mixture over the bottom of a 9×13-inch baking pan. Spread the preserves evenly over the coconut layer. Sprinkle the remaining coconut mixture over the top. Bake at 350 degrees for 25 minutes or until light golden brown. Cool and cut into squares.

YIELD: 35 SQUARES

The great use of life is to spend it for something that outlasts it.
—*William James*

Banana Cream Bars

1½ cups sugar
½ cup (1 stick) butter, softened
2 eggs
¾ cup sour cream
2 teaspoons vanilla extract
2 cups flour

1 teaspoon baking soda
¼ teaspoon salt
2 large or 3 medium bananas, mashed
Cream Cheese Frosting
½ cup chopped nuts (optional)

Cream the sugar and butter in a mixing bowl until light and fluffy. Beat in the eggs. Add the sour cream and vanilla and beat until smooth. Mix the flour, baking soda and salt together. Add to the sour cream mixture alternately with the mashed bananas, mixing until well blended after each addition. Pour into a greased 10×15-inch baking pan. Bake at 350 degrees for 25 to 30 minutes or until brown and the top springs back when lightly touched. Let stand until cool. Spread the Cream Cheese Frosting over the top. Sprinkle with the nuts. Cut into bars.

YIELD: 4 DOZEN

Cream Cheese Frosting

3 ounces cream cheese, softened
6 tablespoons butter, softened
1 tablespoon milk

1 teaspoon vanilla extract
2 cups confectioners' sugar

Combine the cream cheese, butter, milk and vanilla in a mixing bowl and beat until well blended. Add the confectioners' sugar and beat until smooth and creamy.

Butter Balls

½ cup sugar
1 cup (2 sticks) butter or margarine,
    softened
2 teaspoons vanilla extract

2 cups flour
½ teaspoon salt
2½ cups chopped walnuts
Confectioners' sugar

Cream the sugar and butter in a mixing bowl until light and fluffy. Add the vanilla and blend well. Add the flour and salt and mix well. Stir in the walnuts. Refrigerate, covered, overnight. Shape the dough into 1-inch balls and arrange on an ungreased cookie sheet. Bake at 350 degrees for 30 minutes or until light golden brown. Roll the warm cookies in confectioners' sugar to coat well. Place on wire racks to cool.

YIELD: 2 DOZEN

CHEESECAKE SQUARES

1 cup flour
1/3 cup packed brown sugar
1/3 cup butter or margarine, melted
1/2 cup chopped pecans
8 ounces cream cheese, softened

1/4 cup sugar
1 egg
2 tablespoons lemon juice
2 tablespoons milk
1 teaspoon vanilla extract

Combine the flour, brown sugar, melted butter and pecans in a bowl and mix until crumbly. Reserve 1 cup of the mixture for topping. Press the remaining mixture evenly over the bottom of a greased 8-inch square baking pan. Bake at 350 degrees for 10 to 12 minutes or until light brown. Combine the cream cheese and sugar in a mixing bowl and beat until well blended. Add the egg, lemon juice, milk and vanilla and beat until smooth and creamy. Spread over the baked layer. Sprinkle the reserved pecan mixture over the top. Bake at 350 degrees for 25 minutes. Refrigerate until firm. Cut into 2-inch squares.

YIELD: 16 SQUARES

CHOCOLATE CHIP OATMEAL WALNUT COOKIES

1 cup (2 sticks) butter, softened
3/4 cup packed brown sugar
3/4 cup sugar
1 teaspoon baking soda
1 tablespoon warm water
2 eggs

1 teaspoon vanilla extract
1 1/2 cups whole wheat flour
1 teaspoon salt
1 1/2 cups rolled oats
1 to 2 cups chocolate chips
1 cup chopped walnuts

Cream the butter, brown sugar and sugar in a mixing bowl until light and fluffy. Dissolve the baking soda in the warm water in a small bowl. Add the eggs, vanilla extract and dissolved baking soda to the creamed mixture and beat until well blended. Mix the whole wheat flour and salt together and add to the creamed mixture, mixing well. Stir in the oats, chocolate chips and walnuts. Drop by teaspoonfuls onto ungreased cookie sheets. Bake at 350 degrees for 10 to 12 minutes or until brown. Cool on the cookie sheets for 1 to 2 minutes. Remove the cookies to wire racks to cool completely.

YIELD: 4 1/2 DOZEN

BUTTERMILK BROWNIES

2 cups sugar
2 cups flour
1 teaspoon baking soda
1/2 teaspoon salt
1 cup (2 sticks) margarine
1/4 cup baking cocoa

1 cup water
1/2 cup buttermilk
2 eggs
1 teaspoon vanilla extract
Cocoa Buttermilk Frosting

Sift the sugar, flour, baking soda and salt into a large mixing bowl. Melt the margarine in a saucepan. Add the baking cocoa and water and blend well. Bring the mixture to a boil. Add to the dry ingredients and beat until well blended. Add the buttermilk, eggs and vanilla and beat until smooth. Pour into a greased 10×15-inch baking pan. Bake at 350 degrees for 25 minutes or until the brownies pull away from the sides of the pan. Spread the warm Cocoa Buttermilk Frosting over the warm brownies. Cool and cut into squares.

YIELD: 2 DOZEN

COCOA BUTTERMILK FROSTING

1/2 cup (1 stick) margarine
1/4 cup baking cocoa
6 tablespoons buttermilk

1 (1-pound) package confectioners' sugar
1 teaspoon vanilla extract
1 cup chopped walnuts

Melt the margarine in a large saucepan. Add the baking cocoa and buttermilk and blend well. Bring to a boil, stirring frequently and remove from the heat. Add the confectioners' sugar gradually, beating constantly. Beat in the vanilla. Stir in the walnuts.

The better part of one's life consists of his friendships.
—*Abraham Lincoln*

Watch Hill Firehouse Brownies

1 cup (2 sticks) unsalted butter
4 (1-ounce) squares unsweetened
   chocolate
4 eggs
2 cups sugar
1 teaspoon vanilla extract

1 cup flour
1/2 teaspoon salt
1 cup chopped nuts
Confectioners' Sugar Frosting
Chocolate Glaze

Heat the butter and chocolate in a saucepan over medium-low heat until melted and well blended, stirring frequently. Set aside. Beat the eggs in a large mixing bowl. Add the sugar and beat until thick and pale yellow. Blend in the chocolate mixture and the vanilla. Mix the flour and salt together. Add to the chocolate mixture and mix until smooth. Stir in the nuts. Spread the batter in a greased 9×13-inch baking pan. Bake at 325 degrees for 30 to 35 minutes or until the brownies pull away from the sides of the pan. Cool on a wire rack. Spread the Confectioners' Sugar Frosting over the cooled brownies. Drizzle the Chocolate Glaze over the frosted brownies in a decorative pattern. Let stand until the Chocolate Glaze is firm. Cut these rich brownies into small pieces.

YIELD: 4 DOZEN

Confectioners' Sugar Frosting

2 tablespoons butter, softened
1 1/4 cups sifted confectioners' sugar

3 tablespoons light cream

Beat the butter in a small mixing bowl. Add the confectioners' sugar gradually, beating constantly until smooth. Add enough of the cream to make the frosting of spreading consistency.

Chocolate Glaze

2 (1-ounce) squares semisweet chocolate   1 to 2 tablespoons butter

Melt the semisweet chocolate and 1 tablespoon butter together in a small saucepan over low heat, whisking until well blended. Add a small amount of butter if necessary to make a mixture that is pourable.

CHOCOLATE WAFER COOKIES

1 cup sugar
1 cup packed brown sugar
1 cup shortening
4 eggs
1 teaspoon vanilla extract
4 (1-ounce) squares unsweetened
  chocolate, melted
1¹/₃ cups flour

¹/₂ teaspoon salt
¹/₂ teaspoon baking powder
Chopped walnuts (optional)
2 tablespoons margarine, softened
2 cups confectioners' sugar
¹/₈ teaspoon salt
¹/₂ teaspoon vanilla extract
1 to 2 tablespoons milk

Cream the sugar, brown sugar and shortening in a large mixing bowl until light and fluffy. Add the eggs and 1 teaspoon vanilla and beat until well blended. Blend in the melted chocolate. Mix the flour, ¹/₂ teaspoon salt and baking powder together. Add the chocolate mixture and mix well. Stir in the walnuts. Drop by rounded tablespoonfuls onto ungreased cookie sheets. Bake at 350 degrees for 12 to 15 minutes or until dry appearing around the edges and on top. Cool on the cookie sheets for 1 to 2 minutes and remove to wire racks to cool completely. Combine the margarine and remaining ingredients in a small mixing bowl and beat constantly until of spreading consistency. Spread on cookies.

YIELD: 3 DOZEN

CHOCOLATE-DIPPED SHORTBREAD

1¹/₂ cups (3 sticks) butter, softened
³/₄ cup sugar
1 teaspoon vanilla extract
3 cups flour
1 teaspoon salt

Sugar
1 cup semisweet chocolate chips
1 tablespoon shortening
1¹/₂ cups finely chopped nuts (optional)

Combine the butter, ³/₄ cup sugar and vanilla in a mixing bowl and beat until creamy. Add the flour and salt and mix well. Shape by rounded teaspoonfuls into 1-inch balls. Arrange on ungreased cookie sheets and flatten with the bottom of a glass dipped into sugar. Bake at 350 degrees for 10 minutes. Cool on the cookie sheets for 1 to 2 minutes and remove to wire racks to cool completely. Melt the chocolate chips and shortening in a double boiler over hot water, stirring until well blended. Dip each cookie halfway into the melted chocolate, shake off the excess, dip into the nuts and place on waxed paper. Refrigerate for 30 minutes or until the chocolate is set.

YIELD: 5 DOZEN

Coconut Macaroons

2²/₃ cups shredded coconut
²/₃ cup sugar
¹/₄ cup flour

¹/₄ teaspoon salt
4 egg whites
1 teaspoon almond extract

Combine the coconut, sugar, flour and salt in a bowl and mix well. Blend the egg whites with the almond extract in a small bowl. Add the almond mixture to the coconut mixture and stir until moistened. Drop the mixture by rounded tablespoonfuls onto greased cookie sheets. Bake at 325 degrees for 20 to 25 minutes or until the coconut is toasted. Cool on the cookie sheets for 1 to 2 minutes and remove to wire racks to cool completely.

YIELD: 2 DOZEN

Date-Filled Drop Cookies

1 cup shortening
2 cups packed brown sugar
2 eggs
¹/₂ cup buttermilk, sour milk or water
1 teaspoon vanilla extract

3¹/₂ cups flour
1 teaspoon salt
1 teaspoon baking soda
¹/₈ teaspoon cinnamon
Date Filling

Cream the shortening and brown sugar in a mixing bowl until light and fluffy. Add the eggs, buttermilk and vanilla and beat until smooth. Sift the flour, salt, baking soda and cinnamon together. Add the sifted dry ingredients to the egg mixture and mix well. Drop by ¹/₂ teaspoonfuls onto ungreased cookie sheets. Add ¹/₂ teaspoonful of the Date Filling to each and top each with an additional ¹/₂ teaspoonful of the cookie dough. Bake at 350 degrees for 10 to 12 minutes or until golden brown. Cool on the cookie sheets for 1 to 2 minutes. Remove to wire racks to cool completely.

YIELD: 6 DOZEN

Date Filling

2 cups finely chopped dates
³/₄ cup sugar

³/₄ cup water
¹/₂ cup chopped nuts

Combine the dates, sugar and water in a saucepan and cook over medium heat until thickened, stirring constantly. Stir in the nuts. Let stand until cool.

Ginger Cookies

3/4 cup (1 1/2 sticks) melted butter, cooled
1 cup sugar
1/4 cup molasses
1 egg
2 cups flour
2 teaspoons baking soda

1/2 teaspoon cinnamon
1 teaspoon ginger
1 teaspoon mace
1/2 teaspoon cloves
1/2 teaspoon salt
Sugar

Combine the butter, sugar, molasses and egg in a mixing bowl and mix until smooth. Sift the flour, baking soda, cinnamon, ginger, mace, cloves and salt together. Add to the molasses mixture and mix well. Chill the dough, covered, until firm enough to shape. Shape the dough into 1-inch balls and arrange on greased cookie sheets. Flatten the dough with a fork dipped into additional sugar. Bake at 375 degrees for 8 to 10 minutes or until golden brown. Cool on the cookie sheets for 1 to 2 minutes. Remove to wire racks to cool completely.

YIELD: 5 DOZEN

Lemon Bars

2 cups flour
3/4 cup confectioners' sugar
1 cup (2 sticks) margarine
4 eggs
2 cups sugar

1/4 cup flour
1/4 cup lemon juice
Grated peel of 1 lemon
Confectioners' sugar

Mix 2 cups flour and 3/4 cup confectioners' sugar in a bowl. Cut in the margarine until the mixture is crumbly. Press evenly over the bottom of a 9×13-inch baking pan. Bake at 350 degrees for 20 minutes. Beat the eggs in a mixing bowl. Add the sugar and beat until thick and pale yellow. Add the 1/4 cup flour, lemon juice and peel and beat until well blended. Pour over the hot baked layer. Bake at 350 degrees for 20 minutes. Sprinkle with additional confectioners' sugar while warm. Let stand until completely cooled. Cut into bars.

YIELD: 20 BARS

Treat your friends like family and your family like friends.

MEXICAN WEDDING RINGS

1 cup (2 sticks) butter, softened
1/4 cup confectioners' sugar
1 teaspoon vanilla extract

2 cups sifted flour
1 cup chopped walnuts
1 cup (about) confectioners' sugar

Cream the butter and 1/4 cup confectioners' sugar in a mixing bowl until light and fluffy. Beat in the vanilla. Add the flour and walnuts and mix well. Shape the dough into small balls and place on greased cookie sheets. Flatten the balls to the desired size and thickness.

Bake at 300 degrees for 20 minutes or until light golden brown. Place 1 cup confectioners' sugar in a plastic bag. Cool the cookies on the cookie sheets for 1 to 2 minutes. Add the warm cookies 1 or 2 at a time to the confectioners' sugar and shake gently until coated. Place the cookies on wire racks to cool completely.

YIELD: 3 DOZEN

MOLASSES SUGAR COOKIES

This cookie recipe is over 100 years old.

3/4 cup shortening, melted, cooled
1 cup sugar
1/4 cup molasses
1 egg
2 cups flour

2 teaspoons baking soda
1/2 teaspoon salt
1/2 teaspoon cinnamon
1/2 teaspoon ground cloves
Sugar

Combine the shortening, 1 cup sugar, molasses and egg in a mixing bowl and beat until blended. Sift the flour, baking soda, salt, cinnamon and cloves together. Add to the molasses mixture and mix well. Refrigerate, covered, for 1 hour to overnight. Shape the dough into 1-inch balls and roll in sugar to coat. Arrange on greased cookie sheets. Bake at 375 degrees for 8 to 10 minutes. Do not overbake; the centers should be chewy. Cool on the cookie sheets for 1 to 2 minutes and remove to wire racks to cool completely.

YIELD: 3 DOZEN

A loving heart is the truest wisdom.
—*Charles Dickens*

OAT BRAN SQUARES

Varying the ingredients as suggested offers options for different diet preferences but the results are always delicious.

2 cups bran flakes
2 cups old-fashioned oats
1 teaspoon salt
1 1/2 teaspoons baking soda
1 teaspoon cinnamon
1 1/2 cups chopped walnuts

1 to 2 cups chopped dates
4 eggs, beaten or equivalent egg substitute
1 cup honey or dark molasses
1 cup plain yogurt
1 cup vegetable oil or applesauce

Combine the bran flakes, oats, salt, baking soda, cinnamon and walnuts in a large bowl and toss to mix well. Mix in the dates. Beat the eggs in a medium bowl. Add the honey, yogurt and oil and mix well. Add the mixture to the dry ingredients and mix well. Pour into a lightly greased 9×13-inch baking pan. Bake at 325 degrees for 35 to 45 minutes or until firm. Let stand until cool and cut into squares. Especially good served warm with vanilla ice cream.

YIELD: 20 SQUARES

OATMEAL COOKIES

3/4 cup (1 1/2 sticks) margarine, softened
2 cups packed brown sugar
2 eggs
1 teaspoon vanilla extract
1 teaspoon baking soda
2 tablespoons hot water

2 cups flour
1 teaspoon baking powder
1/2 teaspoon salt
3 cups old-fashioned oats
1/3 cup sugar

Cream the margarine and brown sugar in a mixing bowl until light and fluffy. Add the eggs and vanilla and beat until smooth. Dissolve the baking soda in the hot water in a small bowl and add to the brown sugar mixture, blending well. Mix the flour, baking powder and salt together. Add the flour mixture to the brown sugar mixture and mix well. Add the oats and mix well. Shape the dough into small balls and roll in the sugar to coat. Arrange the balls on cookie sheets, leaving space in between for spreading. Bake at 375 degrees for 8 minutes. Cool on the cookie sheets for 1 to 2 minutes. Remove to wire racks to cool completely.

YIELD: 2 DOZEN

Oatmeal Peanut Butter Chocolate Chip Cookies

*If you have trouble deciding if your favorite cookie is oatmeal, chocolate,
or peanut butter, this wonderful cookie covers it all!*

¹/₂ cup (1 stick) margarine, softened	1 teaspoon vanilla extract
¹/₂ cup peanut butter	¹/₂ teaspoon salt
1 cup sugar	¹/₂ teaspoon baking soda
1 cup packed brown sugar	1¹/₂ cups whole wheat flour
¹/₄ cup milk	2¹/₂ cups rolled oats
2 eggs	1 cup semisweet chocolate chips

Blend the margarine and peanut butter in a large mixing bowl. Add the sugar and brown sugar and mix well. Add the milk, eggs and vanilla and mix until well blended. Add the salt, baking soda, flour and oats in the order listed, mixing well after each addition. Stir in the chocolate chips. Drop by tablespoonfuls 2 inches apart onto ungreased cookie sheets. Bake at 350 degrees for about 12 minutes. Cool on the cookie sheets for 1 to 2 minutes and remove to wire racks to cool completely.

YIELD: 6 TO 8 DOZEN

Peanut Butter Bars

¹/₂ cup peanut butter	2 teaspoons vanilla extract
¹/₃ cup margarine, softened	1 cup flour
³/₄ cup packed brown sugar	1 teaspoon baking powder
³/₄ cup sugar	¹/₄ teaspoon salt
2 eggs	1 cup chocolate chips

Combine the peanut butter, margarine, brown sugar and sugar in a mixing bowl and beat until smooth and creamy. Add the eggs and vanilla and beat until well blended. Combine the flour, baking powder and salt. Add the flour mixture to the peanut butter mixture gradually and mix until well blended. Spread the dough in a greased 9×13-inch baking pan. Sprinkle the chocolate chips over the top. Bake at 350 degrees for 5 minutes or until the chocolate chips are melted. Remove the pan from the oven and cut through the melted chocolate chocolate chips and dough with a knife to marbleize. Bake for 25 minutes longer. Place the pan on a wire rack to cool. Cut into 1×2-inch bars.

YIELD: 2¹/₂ DOZEN

CHOCOLATE PEANUT BUTTER BARS

8 ounces (about) graham crackers
1 cup peanut butter
1 (1-pound) package confectioners' sugar

1 cup (2 sticks) margarine, melted
2 cups chocolate chips

Crush the graham crackers into fine crumbs. Combine the crumbs, peanut butter, confectioners' sugar and melted margarine in a large bowl and mix well. Press the mixture evenly into a 10×15-inch baking pan. Place the chocolate chips in a microwave-safe bowl. Microwave until the chocolate chips melt, stirring occasionally. Spread the melted chocolate over the peanut butter layer. Let stand or chill until firm. Cut into bars.

YIELD: 3½ DOZEN

PEANUTTIEST PEANUT BUTTER COOKIES

1 cup peanut butter
1 cup (2 sticks) butter, softened
1 tablespoon vanilla extract
¼ cup maple syrup
2 eggs
1½ cups packed brown sugar
1 cup confectioners' sugar

1½ cups flour
1 cup rolled oats
1 teaspoon baking powder
½ teaspoon salt
1 cup peanut butter chips
½ cup crushed peanuts

Combine the peanut butter, butter, vanilla, maple syrup and eggs in a large mixing bowl and beat until well blended. Add the brown sugar and confectioners' sugar and beat until blended. Mix the flour, oats, baking powder and salt together. Add to the peanut butter mixture and mix well. Stir in the peanut butter chips and crushed peanuts. Shape the dough into desired size balls and arrange on an ungreased cookie sheets. Flatten with a fork in a crisscross pattern. Bake at 350 degrees for 12 to 15 minutes or until brown. Cool on the cookie sheets for 1 to 2 minutes and remove to wire racks to cool completely.

YIELD: 3 DOZEN

When love and skill work together expect a masterpiece.

—*Ruskin*

Rhubarb Bars

1 1/2 cups rolled oats
1 1/2 cups flour
1/4 cup wheat germ
1 cup packed brown sugar

1/2 teaspoon each baking soda and salt
1 cup shortening
1/2 cup chopped nuts (optional)
Rhubarb Filling

Mix the oats, flour, wheat germ, brown sugar, baking soda and salt in a large bowl. Cut in the shortening until crumbly. Add the nuts and mix well. Reserve 1 1/2 cups of the mixture for topping. Press the remaining mixture into a greased 9×13-inch baking pan. Spread the Rhubarb Filling evenly over the oats layer. Sprinkle the reserved oats mixture over the top and press lightly. Bake at 350 degrees for 35 minutes or until golden brown. Cool. Cut into bars.

YIELD: 20 BARS

Rhubarb Filling

3 cups chopped rhubarb
1 1/2 cups sugar
2 tablespoons cornstarch

1/4 cup water
1/2 teaspoon vanilla extract

Combine the rhubarb and sugar in a large saucepan. Dissolve the cornstarch in the water and stir into rhubarb mixture. Bring to a boil, stirring constantly. Cook until thickened, stirring frequently. Remove from the heat and stir in the vanilla. Let stand until cool.

Snickerdoodles

1 cup (2 sticks) butter or margarine,
    softened
1 1/2 cups sugar
2 eggs
1 teaspoon vanilla extract

2 3/4 cups flour
1 teaspoon baking soda
2 teaspoons baking powder
1/4 teaspoon salt
Cinnamon-sugar

Beat the butter and sugar in a mixing bowl until light and fluffy. Beat in the eggs and vanilla. Sift the flour, baking soda, baking powder and salt together. Add to the creamed mixture and mix well. Shape into 1-inch balls and roll in cinnamon-sugar to coat well. Arrange 2 inches apart on ungreased cookie sheets; do not flatten. Bake at 400 degrees for 8 to 10 minutes or until golden brown. Cool on the cookie sheets for 1 to 2 minutes and remove to wire racks to cool completely.

YIELD: 5 TO 6 DOZEN

COOKBOOK CONTRIBUTORS

We at Keepsake Quilting extend our heartfelt thanks to the following members of our quilting family from around the world who enthusiastically shared their recipes with us—from quick-and-easy family favorites to special-occasion dishes. Unfortunately, space limitations prevent us from including all the wonderful recipes received. Our sincere thanks to each and every one of you.

Dorothy Adams
Gina Adams
Christa Afflerbach
Ellen Ahlgren
Susan Aiello
Agnes Alford
Norma Aliah
Kit Allard
Alice Allen
Rebecca Almquist
Nancy Alstad
Mary Altenberg
Charlotte Alvaro
Pamela Andersen
Patricia Anderson
Phyllis Anderson
Judy Applebee
Virlene Arnold
Gloria Arrington
Helen Arrington
Patricia Arrotin
Mary Aslanis
Sandy Asselin
Dorothy Atkinson
Dee Augustin
Jayle Bach
Joann Bailey
Karen Barber
Eunice Barrow
Patricia Bartels
Sally Bates
Judith Battaglia
Barbara Beals
Mrs. Robert Beck
Kimberly Beede
Jacinthe Beguin
Karin Bell
Ginny Belville
Millie Bentley
Jeanne Berard
Susan Berglund
Dee Berkey

Darlene Bernhard
Linda Bevins
Betty Black
Nancy Blackmer
Kathy Blake
Trudi Boehm
Sandra Bonci
Diane Bondar
Debbie Booth
K. Kelly Borowski
Celia Bowen
Cheryl Bowers
Florence Bowers
Debra Bowman
Barbara Boyer
Paula Bradley
Susan Bradshaw
Audrey Bretz
Mary Beth Broderick
Alice Brovold
Martha Brown
Debra Browne
Sharon Brunet
Dawn Buck
Julie Buck
Michael Buck
Helen Bunn
Robin Burghart
Mary Sue Burnham
Dianne Burton
Karen Busch
Patricia Busch
Joan Butcher
Jean Cain
Rita Callahan
Bonnie Camp
Anita Captain
Phyllis Carey
Shirley Carley
Becky Carter
Delores Carvalho
Marjorie Casement

Alice Cassel
Lisa Cazzolli
Jane Chaloner
Martha Chaney
Susan Charbonneau
Cheryl Chase
Cheryl Christensen
Kathy Christensen
Linda Clark
Mary Clark
Sue Clark
Ginger Clarke
Dorothy Clear
Rebecca Clerkin
Terri Clifton
Mary Ann Clover
Lorrie Coats
Laura Coffey
Ernestine Colwell
Mary Comans
Beverly Conway
Thomas Conway
Karen Cook
Amy Cooke
Gaynell Cooper
Pauline Cooper
Teri Cooper
Susanne Corker
Anne Cormier
Ilene Cossey
Dorothy Costa
Judith Cote
Carole Crabtree
Janet Critz
Bernice Croushore
Diane Cychosz
Louise Damiata
Angelia Dappen
Persis Darling
Jean Daugherty
Marie Davies
Jo Ann Day

Elaine Deal
Clarice Dean
Madeleine Debnard
Elaine Decker
Mary Deeney
Michelle DeFour
Margaret DeIntinis
Gloria Delinger
Lorraine Denman
Clyde DeRay
Sue Dicaprio
Phyllis Dill
Lianne Dillon
Jane DiMenno
Beverly Dittus
Dori Dixon
Judy Dixon
Lorayne Dodge
Ann Doherty
Patricia Donnelly
R. Jane Donovan
Kim Drake
Sandy Drake
Ann Drummond-
  Hughes
Abigail Duff
Margaret DuMont
Anne Dunham
Kathy Dunham
Lucy Dunham
Stephanie Dunphy
Winifred Earl
Debbie Eaton
Sue Ebbens
Dorothy Ebi
Carol Eddy
Barbara Edwards
Mary Louise
  Eggimann
Nancy Ekola
Joyce Ellis
Rita English

Phyllis Epping
Lori Essrig
Frances Evans
Mary Farrell
Ann Finney
Dorothy Finsel
Marilyn Fischer
Norma Fleury
Virginia Flynn
Marilyn Follansbee
Nancy Fontaine
Cheryl Forsythe
Patricia Fortner
Catherine Foster
Janice Fox
Marian Fox
Anna Marie Franks
Lois Frantz
Sara Fredette
Jacque Fries
Eleanor Froehlich
Suzanne Frost
Beatrice Fuller
Dorothy Gaither
Donna Galka
Rena Gallup
Linda Galo
Patricia Galvin
Deborah Ganley
Cynthia Garcia
Heidi Gard
Lori Jo Garde
Dolores Gardner
Patricia Garrison
Alice Garves
Agatha Gasaway
Nancy Gates
Susie Gee
Barbara Gerdts
Christine Gevedon
Judy Ghise
Janice Giacoppo

Frances Gilder
Priscilla Golz
Diann Goodger
Barbee Goodman
Irene Goodrich
Sue Goss
Kathy Gottsacker
Mary Lou Grabner
Hilda Graham
Nancy Graham
Patricia Grant
Betty Green
Kim Guinn
Joan Gunder
Mary Gunderson
Pat Habiger
Doris Hall
Judy Hambrick
Darleen Hamburger
Jessie Hamilton
Mary Jean Hammack
Laura Hammond-
    Paden
Linda Hansen
Joleen Hanson
Sue Happ
Kelly Harcus
Paula Hardi
Sharon Harleman-
    Tandy
Bette Harner
Kay Harnishfeger
Dixie Harper
Cheryl Harris
Connie Harrison
Claudia Hart
Joyce Hart
Mamie Hartman
Lorie Hartsig
Fern Harvey
Dorothy Hathaway
Kathleen Hathaway-
    Lloyd
Heather Hatt-Graham
Shirley Haugen
Margie Heidemann
Marlene Heitritter
Beverly Henkel
Betty Hensley
Linda Herche

Natalia Hermosillo
Dee Hervieux
Eleanor Hill
Dean Hix
Stephanie Hlavin-
    Conway
Merrill Hogan-Smith
Ann Holdsworth
Glenva Hollis
Margaret Hood
Elli Horne
Linda Horre
Cindy Hoyt
Ulrike Hubald
Mary Anne Huber
Pat Hudson
Ruby Hundertmark
Barbara Hunter
Shelley Huntoon
Susan Hurley
Barbara Hutcheson
Diane Hutton
Janet Iatridis
Marsha Ifft
Patricia Irwin
Betty Isaac
Barbara Jackson
Lorraine Jackson
Dee Jagerhorn
Frances Jagodzinski
Kathleen Janoff
Mary Jansen-Kubicek
Susan Jaszcz
Beth Jelliffe
Diane Jenkins
Patricia Jensen
Tawna Jensen
Mary Margaret Jewell
Janet Jodrie
Arlene Johnson
Debbie Johnson
Julie Ann Johnson
Marjorie Johnson
Regina Johnson
Beth Jolliffe
Janice Jolly
Anne Jones
Barbara Jones
Lethonee Jones
Melissa Jones-Warner

Marcia Josephson
Audrey Kaiser
Janet Kannady
Anne Kantner
Jennifer Karpa
Kelly Kay
Merlyn Keck
Sherri Keeling
Beverly Keller
Betty Kelley
Leslie Kemp
Joanne Kennedy
Ann Keriazakos
Leslie Kersten
Caroline Kilgore
Kathryn Kimmey
Donna Kincaid
Phyllis King
Rosalie King
Glenda Kirssin
Muriel Klenz
Barbara Klinger
Cara Knight
Bonnie Knott
Eleanore Knott
Eleanor Koester
Dian Kokenge
Jayne Konczakowski
Nancy Kovacs
Echo Kowalzek
Kathy Krogslund
Ruth Kuchinad
Paulette Kusie
Peggy Kwater
Diana LaCount
Lucille LaFlamme
Te Ann Lakeotes
Barbara Lalla
Mili Lamb
Rebecca Lamb
Penny Larango
Patricia Larimer
Linda Laster
Barbara Lauterbach
Marissa Lawrence
Thomas Lebo
Velva Lebo
Debbi LeDonne
Carol Lee
Yvonne Leever

Margaret Lefever
Ruth Legan
Marion Lenaerts
Chris Lesczynski
Lois Lessmann
Juanna Beth Lewis
Sandra Linder
Kay Linehan
Anna Lingwood
Joyce Lloyd
Louise Lochary
Helen Loendorf
Nancy Lofstrand
Mari Lohman
Barbara Lohmann
M. T. Long
Nancy Longley
Cheryl Longyear
Mary Loomis
Mary Losey
Mary Lottman
Jo Loudan
Pam Loveland
Jeryl Lowe
Jill Lowery
Karen Luebbers
Anna Lupkiewicz
Sheryl Lux
Janet Maciolek
Maggie MacPherson
Cynthia Mahdalik
Cindy Mahosky
Hazel Maki
Nancy Manning
Pat Mapa
Laura Marchant
Joyce Markel
Susan Marquardt
Francine Marrs
Andrea Marshall
Cheryl Martin
Helen Martin
Sheila Mason-Gale
Vilma Mathiesen
Sandra Matthijetz
Anna Mattison
Lorraine Matts
Helen Maunu
Penny Maurer
Christine Maybach

Eva Mayfield
Mildred Mayher
Julia Mazurak
Virginia McBride
Cynthia McCarthy
Marilyn McCarthy
Linda McClellan
Becky McClure
Mary Beth
    McCormack
Salena McGalliard
Pamela McHugh
Ruth McHugh
Marcella McIntosh
Rose McKeever
Debbie McMullan
Janet McNary
Betty McNeish
Sharon Meinz
Elaine Melvin
Victoria Menotti
Annette Merrill
Marcy Merrill
Julie Metzger
Haggit Meyer
Rita Micek
Beth Miller
Dyan Miller
Norma Miller
Murri Mills
Elizabeth Mini
Jacquelin Mintal
Dawn Lee Minter
D'Andrea Mitchell
Kaethe Mitchell
Cindy Moore
Marilyn Moorhouse
Donna Moran
Priscilla Moreland
Jan Morin
Ann Morris
Inez Morrison
Karen Morrison
Betty Morton
Joann Moyer
Kay Mullin
Nancy Mullin
Benita Mullis
Peggy Munski
Linda Murphy

Susan Murphy
Shirley Murray
Shirley Nelson
Loraine Nemo
Diane Neri
Barbara Newell
Nancy Newman
Mary Newsome
June Nichols
Gloria Nickolis
Sharon Ninde
Emily Nipp
Karla Nitz
Edith Norcross
Christina Norden
Morena O'Brien
Teresa Okeson-Prater
Hazel Okopinski
Karen Olson
Cyndy O'Malley
Anne O'Neill
Patricia O'Neill
Karan Ortiz
Winifred
    O'Shaughnessy
Nancy Padegenis
Sue Pagan
Barbara Susan Papish
Sharon Paradis-Sharp
Mary Ann Parkhurst
Susan Parrish
Esther Pass
Cathy Pedersen
Linda Pelham
Linda Pelletier
Cecily Perry
Kathleen Peters
MaryAnn Peters
Kathy Petersen
Donna Phelps
Peggy Philippi
Brenda Pichler
Laura Piliaris
Sandy Pizzio
Rita Pollard
Suzanne Pollitt
Rebecca Poole
Mrs. Eugene Posey
Carolyn Postemski
Regie Powell

Anna Prabell
Gabriele Prankel
Iris Price
Jennifer Priebe
Fay Pritts
Judy Proeschel
Joan Prue
Miles Prunier
Olive Prunier
Genevie Przyborski
Margaret Purkey
Irene Pydych
Nancy Quick
Patty Randolph
Diana Reed
Becky Jo Reeves
Anne Regan
Linda Reinagel
Patty Reynolds
Dana Rice
Beverly Richards
Mary Richards
Susan Richardson
Mary Ridder
Gwen Riegel
Dorothy Riggs
Megan Riley
Melba Rilott
Dottie Ritner
Ann Rittal
Regina Roberts
Barbara Robinson
Brenda Robinson
Karren Robinson
Laura Robinson
Jackie Rohrer
Anne Marie Roi
Patsie Ronk
Mae Rene Rose
Melody Rose
Dottie Rotner
Deborah Rubin
Cheryl Rybacki
Judy Sabanek
Patricia Sadeik
Ann Salsbury
Sandy Sanders
Helen Sassen
Darla Sathre
Micheline Satkowski

Marlene Saunders
Hugvette Savoie
Ellen Schaffer
Yvonne Schallenberger
Martha Scheffel
Susan Schiff
Florene Schlueter
Ulrike Schluter-
    Hubald
Julie Schmidt
Margery Schunk
Barbara Schutz
Marie Schwarz
Karen Sebor
Diana Sedler
Carol Seeger
JoAnn Sexton
Mary Jane Sexton
Cheri Shaffer
Ellen Sharp
Marion Shaw
Mary Shaw
Rita Shaw
Julie Shelmandine
JoAnn Shields
Patricia Sievers
Wendy Sikes
Rosie Sinnott
Paula Skinner
Jamie Slater
Cheryl Smith
Gail Smith
Joan Smith
Judith Smith
Leslie Smith
Stephanie Smith
Carole Smolinski
Barbara Snell
Linda Snow
Kathy Solka
Marie Sorensen
Louise Sowers
Arlene Spade
Jan Speicher
Lois Spitler
Linda Spurling
Joan Stacy
Judy Staigmiller
Dawn Stapinski
Sherry Starr

JoAnn Stearns
Shirley Stegmuller
Susan Stemporzewski
Kathy Stencel
Elizabeth Stephenson
Phyllis Sternemann
Jamie Stetler
Fran Stetson
Veronica Stevenson
Cathy Stewart
Kathy Stickney
Anna Stockman
Darcy Stuckey
Iola Sugg
Carolyn Sweetman
Irene Talaasen
Judith Tarentino
Betty Tate
Ethel Terbest
Gina Thackara
Frances Thomas
Elizabeth Thompson
Jacque Thompson
Lois Thompson
Phyllis Thoren
JoAnn Timm
Gail Toerpe
Peggy Tomlinson
Loretta Townsend
Babe Tracey
Carolyn Travers
Rachel Tremblay
Kathy Tripp
Anita Trippi
Mary Troxel
Kim Tucker
Patricia Tye
Mary Umbeck
Beverly Van Cleave
Jan Vandervort
Eleanor Vardanega
Gainor Ventresco
Katherine Vergara
Rhonda Vigness
Janet Visloski
Peggy Voakes
Andrea Vollmer
Donna Waechter
Helen Wakefield
Pat Walter

Carol Wantland
Charla Ward
Valerie Ward
Constance Warren
D. C. Warren
Geneva Watts
Mary Ann Weber
Marjorie Weeman
CiCi Weisbrod
Brenda Weiss
Joyce Weiss
Michele Welles
Mary Lee Westbrook
Patricia Wetzel
Betty Whetton
Debbie Whitcomp
Martha White
Ila Widger
Elaine Wiening
Joyce Wiese
Irma Wilburn
Debra Wilcox
Mary Wiley
Laura Wilhelm
Elizabeth Wilhelmson
Sarah Willette
D. Joan Williams
Dorothy Williams
Hazel Williams
Mary Williams
Rachel Wills
Cathy Wilson
Norma Wilson
Teddy Wintersteen
Carol Woerther
Brenda Wolfe
Steven Wood
Pam Worthen
Margaret Wynn
Julie Yarno
Mollie Yauger
Joy Young
Lois Young
Virginia Young
Ethel Younger
Katherine Zgourides
Jacquelyn Zientek
Mrs. Alvin Zikaras
Kay Zirbel
Barbara Zygiel

INDEX

INDEX

INDEX

INDEX

Route 25B, PO Box 1618
Center Harbor, NH 03226-1618
Phone: 1-800-865-9458 • Fax: 1-603-253-8346
Foreign Orders: Please call 1-603-253-8731

Order Information

Name _____

Address _____

City _____ State _____ Zip _____

Daytime phone ( ) _____ Nightime phone ( ) _____

☐ **Check or Money Order** in U.S. Funds for $_____

☐ **Credit Card Charge to:** ☐ MasterCard ☐ Visa ☐ Discover

Credit card account number:

Expiration date:

/

Signature (required for credit cards only)

Please make check or money order payable to *Keepsake Quilting*.

Photocopies of this form will be accepted.

Please send me _____
copies of the
Keepsake Quilting Cookbook
@ 19.95 each _____

Please send me _____
copies of the
Stargazey Heartz Pattern
@ 10.00 each _____

Postage & Handling $4.99

Total enclosed _____

Route 25B, PO Box 1618
Center Harbor, NH 03226-1618
Phone: 1-800-865-9458 • Fax: 1-603-253-8346
Foreign Orders: Please call 1-603-253-8731

Order Information

Name _____

Address _____

City _____ State _____ Zip _____

Daytime phone ( ) _____ Nightime phone ( ) _____

☐ **Check or Money Order** in U.S. Funds for $_____

☐ **Credit Card Charge to:** ☐ MasterCard ☐ Visa ☐ Discover

Credit card account number:

Expiration date:

/

Signature (required for credit cards only)

Please make check or money order payable to *Keepsake Quilting*.

Photocopies of this form will be accepted.

Please send me _____
copies of the
Keepsake Quilting Cookbook
@ 19.95 each _____

Please send me _____
copies of the
Stargazey Heartz Pattern
@ 10.00 each _____

Postage & Handling $4.99

Total enclosed _____